John Pilkington Norris

A Key to the Narrative of the four Gospels

John Pilkington Norris

A Key to the Narrative of the four Gospels

ISBN/EAN: 9783743349926

Manufactured in Europe, USA, Canada, Australia, Japa

Cover: Foto ©ninafisch / pixelio.de

Manufactured and distributed by brebook publishing software (www.brebook.com)

John Pilkington Norris

A Key to the Narrative of the four Gospels

A KEY

TO THE GOSPEL NARRATIVE

RIVINGTONS

𝕷onbon..............................*Waterloo Place*
𝕺xforb........ ....*High Street*
𝕮ambridge..............................*Trinity Street*

A KEY

To the Narrative of

THE FOUR GOSPELS

BY JOHN PILKINGTON NORRIS, M.A.

CANON OF BRISTOL, AND FORMERLY ONE OF H. M. INSPECTORS OF SCHOOLS

RIVINGTONS

London, Oxford, and Cambridge

1869

Preface

THIS is an age of historical criticism. Some think we are carrying it too far. It is difficult to see how it can possibly be carried too far, so long as it is sincere and thoroughgoing. But, rightly or wrongly, so it is. Everything purporting to be a fact in the world's history is being thus tested, that we may see for ourselves whether it have about it the character of an authentic fact or no. The Gospel narratives cannot escape this kind of criticism.

The purpose of the following pages is to help our younger students to realize to themselves the narrative of these four Gospels : to show that they are not *contradictory* but *supplemental* to each other.

It may not be possible to weave into one consistent chronicle *all* their anecdotes of our blessed Lord's ministry. But it may be possible so far to succeed in reconstructing the original order of events, as to satisfy any candid mind that their discrepancies are only such as might naturally be expected in four independent portraitures; and to quicken the reader's consciousness of the *reality* of the Divine original.

This last is the all-important thing. We may or we may not be able to answer all the cavils of one who is unwilling to receive the truth. But to strengthen our own convictions, to learn to read these records of Christ with a vivid perception of their intense truthfulness, to freshen and deepen those impressions which long familiarity may have weakened, this is of infinite concern, if to know Him be indeed to us eternal life.

Contents

PART I

The Four Gospels

CHAP.		PAGE
I.	EXTERNAL TESTIMONIES TO THEIR AUTHENTICITY	1
II.	THEIR INTERNAL CHARACTER	10

PART II

The Gospel Narrative

I.	BIRTH AND YOUTH OF OUR LORD	18
II.	BAPTISM, TEMPTATION, AND FIRST YEAR'S MINISTRY	23
III.	SECOND YEAR, FIRST QUARTER—THE GREAT GALILEAN MINISTRY	30
IV.	SECOND YEAR, SECOND QUARTER—PASSOVER AND NORTHERN TOUR	38
V.	SECOND YEAR, THIRD QUARTER—TRANSFIGURATION AND FEAST OF TABERNACLES	46
VI.	SECOND YEAR, FOURTH QUARTER—FINAL RETURN TO JUDEA, AND FEAST OF DEDICATION	52

CHAP.		PAGE
VII.	THIRD YEAR, FIRST QUARTER—RAISING OF LAZARUS, AND FINAL ASCENT TO JERUSALEM	57
VIII.	EARLY DAYS OF HOLY WEEK	63
IX.	THE LAST SUPPER AND THE BETRAYAL	72
X.	JUDGMENT IN THE JEWISH COURT	78
XI.	JUDGMENT IN THE ROMAN COURT	83
XII.	THE CRUCIFIXION	89
XIII.	THE BURIAL AND RESURRECTION	95
XIV.	THE FORTY DAYS	101

PART III

Notes on the Gospel Narrative

I.	ON THE NARRATIVE OF THE BIRTH AND INFANCY	108
II.	ON THE SILENCE OF THE GOSPELS RESPECTING OUR LORD'S LIFE AT NAZARETH	112
III.	ON THE NARRATIVE OF THE TEMPTATION	115
IV.	ON OUR LORD'S MIRACLES	119
V.	CHRIST'S DEATH A MYSTERY	127
VI.	ON THE CHRONOLOGY OF THE GOSPEL NARRATIVE	132

PART I
The Four Gospels

CHAPTER I
External Testimonies to their Authenticity

NO fact in the world's history is more certain than that 1800 years ago, in the broad daylight of the Roman Empire, there came into existence, and rapidly increased in numbers, a society of men calling themselves Christians.

The Roman historian of the period[1], writing with a strong heathen prejudice, mentions them by name, and adds that 'their founder was one *Christus*, who suffered capital punishment under the procurator Pontius Pilate, in the reign of Tiberius; but that this mischievous superstition, repressed for a while, burst forth again, not only throughout Judea, where it first arose, but even in Rome.'

And then he goes on to describe how Nero charged them with having set fire to Rome, and tried to crush them by persecution. This was A.D. 64.

Forty years later, the accomplished Pliny found such multitudes professing Christianity in Asia Minor, that the temples of the heathen gods were deserted; and we have a letter from him to the Emperor Trajan, asking how he was to deal with them, and de-

[1] Tacitus, *Ann.* xv. 44.

scribing their habits,—how 'they assembled on certain stated days before it was light, and repeated in alternate verses one with another a hymn or form of prayer to Christ, as to some God, binding themselves by a sacrament[1],—not for any criminal purpose—but to abstain from fraud, theft, and adultery, from falsifying their word, from retaining what did not belong to them[2]; after which it was their custom to separate, and then reassemble to eat in common a harmless meal.'

This, he said, had been going on for twenty years or more.

In vain the Roman magistrates tried to trample out this 'new superstition.' The more they crushed it, the more it grew; and two centuries later it became the state-religion of the Empire.

All this is mere matter of notoriety, not resting on the authority of the Christians or their writings, nor belonging to any dark ages of the world's history, but recorded in the contemporary annals of the Roman Empire in the days of its greatest splendour.

Deeply interesting it must be, from even a merely historical point of view, to inquire what account these Christians gave of themselves and of their origin.

An anecdote has been preserved which may serve to illustrate the unobtrusiveness and modesty of the early Christians when called upon to give an account of themselves :—

About fifteen years before the date of Pliny's letter, the Emperor Domitian was alarmed by the revival of a report which had been very prevalent at the beginning of his father's reign, that a great prince was

---

[1] Pliny would doubtless understand by this an oath merely.
[2] May we not recognise here the latter commandments of the Decalogue?

expected to appear in Judea, and that he was to come from the house of David. He ordered inquiry to be made in Palestine for any descendants of David, and two sons (or grandsons) of Jude ('the Lord's brother') were brought before him. 'He demanded whether they were descended from David. They confessed it. Again he inquired what were their means. They declared that they possessed but 9000 denarii (about £300), and a few acres of land in Judea. They showed him their hands, hard with daily toil, in token of the simple industry by which they gained their living. Once more the Emperor asked what was the meaning of *Christ's kingdom*, to which they replied that *it was not of this world, but should appear at the consummation of all things*. Domitian, it is said, was satisfied with these answers; and, it is added, put a stop from that moment to the persecution of the Christians.'—(Merivale's *History of Rome*, chap. lxii.)

This harmlessness and entire absence of worldly ambition appear in the public 'Apologies,' which from time to time the Christians addressed to the Imperial Government. But in these same Apologies there appears also—what the Romans could not comprehend or forgive—their deep enthusiastic reverence for Christ their Founder; their intense conviction that He was living in the unseen world, and daily pouring His Holy Spirit into their hearts; their ardent expectation of His near return to judge the world.

But what had their Founder done, or what had He left behind Him on the earth to explain all this?

He left no writings[1]. He had simply left behind

---

[1] Augustine thinks it necessary to explain the reasons of this at great length in his book *De Consensu Evangelistarum*.

Him a group of men on whom He had made so deep an impression that their whole character was changed, and they were fired with a holy zeal to work in others that same change of which they were so conscious in themselves.

Christianity was to them not a doctrine merely, not a record, but a *life*[1], a new vital principle throbbing in every pulse of their being, which they felt bound to impart to others also, to as many as they could reach, before the second coming of their Lord. The precious memory of all that Christ had said and done and suffered, while on earth, lived from mouth to mouth, was the staple of their preaching, was the first lesson of their catechumens. 'The time was so short'[2] that it seemed hardly necessary to stamp with official authority any of the written records of these facts.

But in the next generation, when Christ's return was still delayed, and seemed likely to be delayed, and when the growth of erroneous notions made an appeal to some written rule of faith a necessity, the Christians began carefully to treasure and transcribe such memoirs of Christ as the Apostles or their companions had committed to writing for the use of any of their converts.

Thus it happened that whereas the earlier Christians appealed to the facts of Christ's ministry as known by oral tradition, saying, 'It has been delivered to us by those who were eye-witnesses,' or the like,—a later generation, beginning with Justin Martyr, began to appeal to written documents.

In Justin Martyr we find such an appeal repeatedly. He wrote his Dialogue and his Apology between the years 140 and 150 A.D. He was of Greek descent,

---

[1] Acts v. 20.   [2] 1 Cor. vii. 29.

born near the ancient Shechem. After trying all the schools of Philosophy, and finding them unsatisfactory, he was led by a meek and venerable old man, whom he met one day on the sea-shore, to embrace Christianity. 'Many things,' he says, 'this old man told me which I cannot now record. I saw him no more. But forthwith a fire was kindled in my soul, and I was filled with a love of those prophets and friends of Christ of whom he had spoken. And when I pondered all his words, I began to see that this was the only philosophy which was safe, and suited to my need.'

Twelve times Justin refers to the written *Memoirs* of the Apostles, as he calls them ; and that by these 'Memoirs' he meant our four Gospels, is rendered highly probable by the fact that wherever he quotes them—and he makes *seven* such quotations—the words are to be found in one or other of our Gospels.

In his famous account of the Christian Eucharist[1], he says, 'The Apostles, in Memoirs which they wrote, and which are called Gospels, have recorded these injunctions of the Lord.' And in the same passage he tells us how the Christians of the country villages assembled together every Sunday to hear the Memoirs of the Apostles, or the books of the Prophets, read aloud. And again in his Dialogue[2] he writes :—'In the Memoirs, which I say were composed by the Apostles and their companions, we read that sweat as drops streamed down from Him, as He was praying and saying, Let this cup pass from me.' That by 'the followers of the Apostles' he here alluded specially to St. Luke, is very clear, not only because the passage quoted occurs in St. Luke, but also because

[1] *Apol.* i. 66, 67. [2] Ch. 103.

the Greek word used for 'follower' is the very word by which St. Luke describes himself in the preface to his Gospel.

Papias, a contemporary of Justin, mentions the Gospels of St. Matthew and St. Mark by name. He was the friend of Polycarp, and, like him, is said to have been a disciple of St. John. In his work, *An Exposition of the Oracles of the Lord*, of which fragments have been preserved to us in Eusebius[1], he says, 'Matthew composed his *oracles* in Hebrew, and each one interpreted them as he was able.' Of St. Mark he says, 'Mark having become Peter's interpreter, wrote accurately all that he remembered; though he did not record in order that which was said or done by Christ. For he neither heard the Lord, nor followed Him; but subsequently, as I said, attached himself to Peter, who used to frame his teaching to meet the immediate wants of his hearers; and not making a connected narrative of the Lord's discourses.' He seems too in another fragment to quote St. John.

Either Papias or some contemporary—certainly not later than A.D. 170—wrote a complete *Canon* of the Books of the New Testament as then received in the Christian Church. A precious fragment of this Canon was discovered in the Ambrosian Library at Milan, and was published in 1740, by Muratori. It is sadly mutilated, but enough remains to give it the highest value.

Mr. Westcott (in his *History of the New Testament Canon*) thus gives its substance:—

'The fragment commences with the last words of a sentence which evidently referred to the Gospel of St. Mark. The Gospel of St. Luke, it is then said, stands

[1] *Ecc. Hist.* iii. 39.

third in order, having been written by Luke the Physician, St. Paul's companion, who not being himself an eye-witness, based his narrative on such information as he could obtain, beginning from the birth of the Baptist. The fourth place is given to the Gospel of St. John, a disciple of our Lord ; and the occasion of its writing is thus described : In reply to the entreaties of his fellow-disciples and bishops John said, " Fast with me for three days from this time, and whatever shall be revealed to each of us, whether it be favourable to my writing or not, let us relate it one to another." On the same night it was revealed to Andrew, one of the Apostles, that John should relate all things in his own name, aided by the revision of all. What wonder is it then that John so constantly brings forward Gospel-phrases, even in his Epistles, saying in his own person, " What we have seen with our eyes, and heard with our ears, and our hands have handled, these things have we written"? For so he professes that he was not only an eye-witness, but also a hearer, and moreover a historian of all the wonderful works of our Lord.'

Though the beginning of this fragment has been destroyed, there can be no doubt that St. Matthew occupied the first place in his Canon. Further on he thus affirms distinctly the Church's belief in their inspiration :—' Though various points are taught in each of the Gospels, it makes no difference to the faith of believers, since in all of them all things are declared by one overruling Spirit[1] concerning the Nativity, the Passion, His conversation with His disciples, and His double advent, at first in humility, and afterwards in royal power as He will yet appear.' The writer of the manuscript then mentions the Acts, thirteen Epistles of

[1] ' Uno ac principali spū declarata.'

St. Paul, and other books, some of which the Church judged afterwards to be Apocryphal.

Irenæus, writing to his friend Florinus (about A.D. 177), and fondly recalling his intercourse in earlier days with Polycarp, alludes to the four Gospels under the well-understood title of Scriptures[1]. The passage is too interesting to be abridged :—

'I well recollect seeing thee in Asia Minor, at the house of Polycarp, when I was a boy, and thou wast in attendance on Hadrian's court, and seeking to commend thyself to Polycarp. Indeed, the events of my boyhood I remember better than what is more recent. For what is then put into our memory seems to grow with our growth, and become part of our very being. I could describe the exact spot where the blessed Polycarp used to sit and converse ; his goings-forth and his comings-in ; the whole manner of his life, and his personal appearance ; I remember his discourses to the people, and how he would narrate his intercourse with John and with the others who had beheld the Lord ; and how he repeated their words, and what he had heard from their lips about the Lord and about His miracles and teaching ; all this, received directly from those who were eye-witnesses of the Word of Life, used Polycarp to relate, *agreeing throughout with the Scriptures*'[2].

This same Irenæus, in his book 'Against Heresies' (iii. 1), speaks of the Gospel which the Apostles first preached orally, and afterwards *by the will of God* handed down to us in a written form, 'the foundation and pillar of our faith.' And again in the 12th chap-

---

[1] Compare Matt. xxvi. 54, Luke xxiv. 27, Acts xviii. 28, 1 Cor. xv. 3, 4, and 2 Peter iii. 16, where the term seems to be applied to St. Paul's Epistles.

[2] *Fragmenta Irenæi* (Stieren's edition, vol. i. p. 822).

ter he says, 'Whence it appears that the all-creating Word, who sitteth between the cherubim, and holdeth together all things, hath given us the Gospel, fourfold in form, but held together by one Spirit.'

In the second book his language is as strong as can well be about the inspiration of the Evangelists. After expressly defining 'Scripture' to mean the writings both of prophets and evangelists in the 27th chapter, he says in the 28th that where we find difficulties we must assume the fault to be in ourselves, 'because the Scriptures, being spoken by the Word and Spirit of God, are perfect.'

Thus it appears that within a hundred years of the fall of Jerusalem, and almost within the lifetime of disciples of one of the Apostles, the Christian Church had accepted and stamped with the seal of inspiration these four Gospels, as the only authoritative records of our Lord's sojourn upon earth.

From this time forward these four written Gospels came to be considered the most precious treasures of the Christian Church. Copies of them were multiplied, and they were bound up with the other sacred books. By the good providence of God two of these manuscript copies, both written before the close of the fourth century, have been preserved down to our own time. One is in the Vatican library at Rome, the other (discovered in the monastery of Mount Sinai, ten years ago) is in the Imperial library at St. Petersburg. A third, of equal authority, written apparently early in the fifth century, is in the British Museum. Few, if any, books of ancient times have come down to us so authenticated by external testimony as these four Gospel narratives of our blessed Lord's sojourn upon earth.

CHAPTER II

Their Internal Character

WE open these Gospels and read them, and what do we find?

Four brief narratives, none of them longer than a modern pamphlet, none of them a complete biography, but each one rather a collection of salient anecdotes and discourses, precisely such as an earnest preacher would select in order to convey to his hearers in the shortest compass a vivid portraiture of Him whom he wished to make known to them. They have much, necessarily, in common: all proceed upon one main outline of facts—the Baptism, the Ministry, the details of the Condemnation and Crucifixion, the Resurrection of our Lord.

And yet how distinct are these four portraitures! And above all, what a marked difference between the three earlier Gospels and the fourth! Of this latter and most obvious difference let us first speak,—the difference between St. John's Gospel and the rest.

The first three Evangelists, until they come to the final journey to Jerusalem, narrate only what occurred in Galilee. Whereas St. John's narrative to the extent of six-sevenths of its space has Jerusalem for its scene.

Again, the three Galilean Gospels (as we may call them) have many miracles, many parables in common; told sometimes in almost identical words, as though they had derived their narrative from the often repeated oral teaching of the self-same eye-witnesses (and this may well be the explanation). St. John, on the contrary, relates no parables, and has but one miracle in common with the rest.

Again, the Three relate chiefly our Lord's popular discourses concerning His Kingdom; St. John for the most part His conversations with the Apostles or controversies with the Jews about His own Person and Mission.

But the difference in style is still more striking. The Three write a plain narrative, making no comment, never speaking in their own person (except in St. Luke's brief preface); St. John writes authoritatively, theologically, enforcing his own explanation of the facts which he relates.

These contrasts, which so widely separate the fourth Gospel from the rest, are at once explained by the fact which the early Church traditions unanimously affirm, that St. John wrote thirty years later than the rest, for a generation of men who had grown up in the Christian faith, and been familiar from childhood with that more popular cycle of Apostolic teaching which the three earlier Evangelists had embodied in their Gospels. We may accept or reject the anecdote preserved by Eusebius (*Ecc. Hist.* iii. 24), that the elders of Ephesus brought the three earlier Gospels under the special attention of the aged Apostle, and that he approved them, only noticing that some things were yet wanting, and wrote his own Gospel by way of supplement to them[1]; but one thing is certain, that,

---

[1] Dr. Routh, in a note on Muratori's Fragment, speaks without any doubt of the authenticity of this anecdote of the primitive Church.—*Rel. Sac.* i. 407.

if not these actual Gospels, yet at any rate *their substance*, as repeated over and over again by the Apostles and their ministers in preparing catechumens for baptism, was already familiar to the readers for whom St. John wrote. Hence (what otherwise would be inexplicable) his silence respecting such events as the Ascension and Transfiguration, and the institution of the Eucharist, of each of which, however (as has been well observed), he seems to assume a knowledge in his readers' minds [1].

Setting apart, therefore, this fourth Gospel as possessing a character of its own altogether distinct from that of the rest, we proceed to consider the other three. And here too, in the midst of much general agreement, we find differences,—traces of three distinct cycles of oral teaching, as though addressed to three distinct groups of Christian Churches.

We read St. Matthew's Gospel from end to end continuously, so as to gather one general impression; we mark the pedigree from *Abraham*, the father of God's chosen people; the call from Egypt, as with Israel of old, so with the Hope of Israel; the ever recurring appeal to the Old Testament; the careful notice of every minute accomplishment of Messianic prophecy; the stress laid on Christ's fulfilment of the Law [2]; the repeated announcement that a restoration of the theocratic kingdom was at hand; the number of parables specially explaining the nature of this kingdom;—we cannot mark all these characteristics

[1] For St. John's allusions to the Ascension, see vi. 62; to the Transfiguration, i. 14 (comparing 2 Pet. i. 17, and noticing the phrase 'the only begotten of the Father,' in which there seems to be a reference to the Voice then heard); to the Eucharist, xiii. 2.

[2] Matt. ii. 15; v. 17.

without recognising the truth of the Church's constant tradition that this Gospel was specially addressed to the people of Israel. St. Matthew wrote to persuade God's people that in Jesus of Nazareth whom they had crucified, they might indeed confess the Prophet like unto Moses, the true Son of David, the restorer of His kingdom, the Messiah of all prophecy.

We pass on to St. Mark, and we find that his Gospel is far from being (as St. Augustine so hastily asserted[1]) a mere abbreviation of St. Matthew's. There are incidents in our Lord's ministry that we know from St. Mark, and St. Mark only,—the intervention of His family (iii. 20, 21), the parable of the seed growing secretly (iv. 26-29), the healing of the deaf man of Decapolis (vii. 31-37), and of the blind man of Bethsaida (viii. 22-26), the name of Bartimeus (x. 46), and of Simon of Cyrene's sons (xv. 21), the young man's flight at Gethsemane (xiv. 51, 52).

Besides this we have many vivid touches in the narrative, clearly due to an eye-witness—wanting in St. Matthew,—as in the account of the Gadarene demoniac, and of the Transfiguration. Four times he alone of the Evangelists notices our Lord's look (iii. 34, viii. 33, x. 21, 23). May we not in this greater vividness of detail recognise the aid of St. Peter, under whose direction the later Christians believed the Gospel to have been written? That it was written, if not at Rome, yet for Romans, is rendered probable by the constant use of Latin words, the careful explanation of Jewish terms and usages, and the rare reference to the Old Testament. It is a Gospel more of facts than of discourses, of action more than of reflection, suited to the Roman genius; it is as though he wished above all

[1] *De Consensu Evang.* i. 1.

things to portray Christ as more than man, instinct with divine creative energy, the Lord of Nature; or, as he himself puts it, 'The Gospel of Jesus Christ the Son of God.'

Lastly, we turn to St. Luke, and notice how (in complete contrast to St. Mark) the gradual unfolding and growth of our Lord's humanity are traced through birth and infancy and boyhood; how in the ministry every detail is brought forward that reveals the human sympathies of Christ, His sympathies not so much with the Israelite, as with man as man,—'touched with a feeling of our infirmities;' reclaiming the prodigal, seeking the lost sheep, the good Samaritan and friend of all who need Him,—of the widow of Nain, of the dying thief; we notice how the very pedigree, unlike St. Matthew's, proclaims the *universality* of Christ's mission, tracing back His descent not to Abraham only, but to Adam. Can any fail to recognise in this picture the Redeemer, the Mediator, the High Priest of the whole human race? Can any doubt the truth of the uniform testimony of the Fathers that St. Luke wrote under the influence of the Apostle of the Gentiles, for those Greek Churches of which St. Paul was the founder?

How entirely this agrees with what we hear in the Acts and Epistles of their companionship, and with the striking coincidence of St. Luke's narrative of the last supper with St. Paul's account of its institution to the Corinthians!

It is important to realize to the full the distinctness of these four portraitures :—Christ the Messiah of Israel, Christ the mighty Lord of Nature, Christ the Friend and Priest of all mankind, Christ the true Light and Life of the World. Fourfold our Gospel must ever be, fourfold as those streams of Eden, fourfold as those living creatures of the Apostle's Vision, fourfold as the divine character of Him whom these Evangelists reveal to us. If to know Him in all His fulness be indeed to us eternal life, we cannot afford to merge in one these separate aspects of our Lord. Instead of wondering at their differences, may we not rather bless and praise God for them?

No *harmony*, however perfect, can ever have a value at all approaching the value of these four originals.

Why then attempt such a narrative as that which follows?

Two reasons may be given.

The first is, that modern criticism will not let these Gospels rest. If they be not only diverse in character, but also contradictory, irreconcilable, clearly their credibility is so far invalidated. How then can this be best tested?

If we had before us four separate ancient pictures, purporting to represent severally the north, east, south, and west aspects of some stately temple no longer standing: and they seemed at first sight so unlike each other, that it was questioned whether they could really be what they professed,—how might their credibility be best proved? Obviously, if they were true and authentic, then a model might be constructed having four such sides, which would at the same time be seen to form one consistent whole,— rough and incomparably inferior in beauty to the four ancient pictures, but still fulfilling its special purpose usefully.

So with these four Gospels:—if we can really construct a narrative of events such as might well form a basis of fact for each one of the four, then all doubt of their credibility on the score of their discrepancies would be removed.

Nor need this be done perfectly or exhaustively. To any candid mind it will be enough if a sufficiently near approach be made to such a narrative as to suggest the probability that *if we knew all* it might easily be perfected.

Not knowing all, any such reconstruction of the order of events must be to some extent conjectural. None of the three earlier Evangelists appear to follow a strict chronological order in their narratives of the Galilean ministry. Some group kindred parables together, some group miracles. The healing of the Gadarene demoniac is placed by St. Mark after a whole cycle of events which in St. Matthew precede it. Much of St. Matthew's Sermon on the Mount is to be found in St. Luke in the chapters that follow the Transfiguration. The Supper at Bethany, which St. John tells us clearly took place before Palm Sunday, is by the three other Evangelists told after the events of Tuesday in Holy week, apparently because they connected it in their minds with Judas's treachery.

To one who rightly understands the view with which they wrote, intending to give not a biography but a portraiture of our blessed Lord, all this will rather increase than lessen his belief that they wrote under the superintendence of the Holy Spirit. God's purpose was not that we should know all about Christ, but that we should know Him; and for this far higher purpose, groups of anecdotes so arranged as best to illustrate His teaching and His character, were more likely to be effective than any mere chronicle from month to month. For this higher purpose we must ever have recourse to the inspired originals. For that other lower purpose such a compilation as the present may be useful.

But there is another and a stronger motive. We can never truly appreciate the individuality of the originals until we have tried thus to co-ordinate them. Nothing helps to quicken the student's enjoyment of these four Gospels, each in its own special character, more effectually than having once, at all events, gone through this process of collating them one with another in four parallel columns, as it were, and so been led to make out for himself all their latent harmonies. One Gospel will be found to throw light on another in a hundred ways that would never otherwise be suspected. And as in that beautiful invention of modern days, in which by combining into one focus two slightly varying aspects of a view, we gain a depth of perspective, and a solidity of form that seems to bring the very original before us; so here, by stereoscoping into one view these four aspects of our blessed Lord, we may enable ourselves to see greater *reality* in that divine image which each one separately sets forth.

PART II
The Gospel Narrative

CHAPTER I
Birth and Youth of Our Lord

IT was in the village of Nazareth, among the green hills of Galilee, that Mary was living, still in her own home; for though she was betrothed to Joseph, and had pledged to him her faith, yet, according to the custom of Jewish maidens, she would remain a twelvemonth longer under her parents' roof. It was during this period that the angel Gabriel appeared to her, and told her that she should conceive and bring forth a son, and that her son should be the Messiah. A child without a father! Mary trembled at the mystery: but the angel revealed all :—'That holy thing that shall be born of thee shall be the Son of God!'

Brief as was the interview, the angel left her not without a token, whereby, when he was gone, she might ascertain assuredly that this was no illusion :— 'Thy cousin Elisabeth hath conceived, and shall also bear a son.'

To her cousin Elisabeth at Hebron Mary hastens, a four days' journey, a hundred miles or more; and it is even so. Nay, and the aged Elisabeth is inspired to greet her as the mother of her Lord. Mary's heart is full, filled with the prophetic inspiration of her race, and she pours forth the hymn that Christians have ever since loved to chant in their evening worship.

Three months, or nearly up to the birth of Elisabeth's child, she remained her guest; and then returned to her Galilean home. *Then*, it must have been, on her return, that Joseph's mind was troubled with perplexing doubts. But to him too God revealed it all. And the days of betrothal being ended, he took Mary to his house. But can it be that the Son of David should be born away from David's city! No: God's Providence is so ordering it that every prophecy shall be fulfilled; and to Bethlehem both Joseph and Mary are summoned,—both being of the tribe and lineage of David,—for the enrolment which the Roman Emperor had ordered.

There, sheltered for the night in one of the limestone caverns just outside the town, where the peasants stalled their cattle,—so Justin Martyr was told little more than a hundred years afterwards, doubtless by the natives of the place[1],—the virgin mother gave birth to her promised child. She well remembered in after years, how, as she lay in her weakness, the gentle shepherds came with eager haste, telling of the great light, and of the angel's message of great joy, and wishing to see the Child who was to be their Saviour.

Comparing our two accounts we may infer that Joseph now made Bethlehem his home. There on the eighth day the Babe was circumcised, and named Jesus, as the angel had commanded.

Forty days after the nativity, according to the law

[1] *Dial.* c. 78.

of Moses, the days for the mother's purification being accomplished, they take the holy Babe up to Jerusalem (six miles from Bethlehem), and there in the Temple 'present Him to the Lord.' Nor were worshippers wanting when the infant Messiah thus appeared for the first time in His Father's Temple. Holy Simeon was there, and taking the Child in his arms poured forth his prophetic psalm. The daughter of Phanuel was there also, the widowed prophetess, lifting up her voice in praise, and speaking of the child to all who like herself were looking for redemption in Jerusalem.

Soon after this Presentation, probably, there arrived in Jerusalem those strange visitors from the East. Magi, or Wise men, they are called,—a priestly caste of the Medes and Persians, of whom we read much in the Book of Daniel; Daniel was made master of the Magicians and Astrologers,—possibly from him they had derived their expectation of the Jewish Messiah. Through their knowledge of the stars God revealed to them that the fulness of time was come : the mystic weeks of their great master Daniel were fulfilled. No wonder all Jerusalem was excited; no wonder the usurper Herod trembled for his throne. The Sanhedrim was summoned; the sacred books consulted; at Bethlehem the Holy Child, if really born, is to be found. Thither the Chaldæan embassy repair with their gifts of homage. Thither the incensed tyrant sends his murderous agents to destroy the Child. Surely (the king thought) if all born within two years are slain, this so-called Messiah cannot escape. But already—warned by God's angel in a dream—the faithful Joseph, under cover of the night, was far upon the road to Egypt with the young Child and His mother.

This must have been in February, just when the

dying tyrant was seeking the baths of Jericho, there to spend the last six weeks of his miserable life. In the first week of April the angel reappeared, according to his promise, to tell Joseph of Herod's death; and they retraced their steps towards Bethlehem, their adopted home. But when Joseph 'heard that Archelaus did reign in Judea in the room of his father Herod, he was afraid to return thither: and[1] being warned of God in a dream, turned aside into Galilee,' and once more made Nazareth his abode.

And here a veil falls over that sacred home. For well-nigh thirty years—with one brief exception—the life of Him who was 'the desire of all nations' is hidden from us. We only know that behind that veil 'the Child grew, and waxed strong in spirit, filled with wisdom; and the grace of God was upon Him.'

Once, and once only, that veil is lifted, and we are permitted to behold Him, a Boy of twelve years, accompanying His mother and Joseph in their annual journey to Jerusalem at the Paschal season. Eight days the feast lasted; 'and when they had fulfilled the days, as they returned, the Child Jesus tarried behind in Jerusalem, and Joseph and His mother knew not of it.' The caravan of pilgrims was a large one, and they had kinsfolk in it; might He not well be with them? But no; their search is in vain. So Joseph and Mary, 'sorrowing,' retrace their steps. Two whole days are spent in the crowded city seeking Him. On the third they find Him in one of the schools or lecture-rooms, apparently, that opened into the Temple cloister, where the Jewish professors held their disputations and taught their classes. And

[1] The word 'notwithstanding' in our English Version is not in the original, and spoils the sense.

there Mary finds her Son, 'sitting among the doctors, both hearing them and asking them questions.' It would seem as though she paused, afraid to interrupt —paused long enough to note the admiration with which these Rabbis were regarding her Son. But when all is over, and they are alone with Him, Mary speaks. We must observe this—it is Mary alone who claims authority over Him—the mystery of His birth seems tacitly acknowledged in the prominence conceded to Mary ; and yet, how naturally (such being, doubtless, the custom of her household) she speaks of Joseph as 'Thy father,'—'Son, why hast Thou thus dealt with us ? behold, Thy father and I have sought Thee sorrowing.' So Mary, most naturally ; but mark the dawning consciousness of the higher Sonship in the answer, 'How is it that ye sought Me ? wist ye not that I must be in the precincts of My Father ?'— for such seems to be the right translation, in the courts or precincts of My Father's house. But let that be : observe only how mysteriously, and yet how naturally also, how instinctively in the depth of His own divine consciousness, Jesus speaks of Himself, at twelve years old, as the Son of God ! As the Son of God, and yet in all things willing 'to learn obedience'[1]; for ' He went down with them, and came to Nazareth, and was subject unto them.'

And here once more the curtain falls ; and for eighteen long years the life of the youthful Messiah is veiled from view. It is not yet time for 'the arm of the Lord' to be revealed. He must 'grow up as a tender plant,' secluded from our curious eye :—enough for us to know that He was 'increasing in wisdom and stature, and in favour with God and man.'

[1] Heb. v. 8.

CHAPTER II

Baptism, Temptation, and First Year's Ministry

IT was at the commencement of His thirty-first year, in the month of February, so far as we can gather from St. Luke's careful date, that Jesus left His humble home at Nazareth, and mingled, an unknown stranger, with the crowd who flocked to hear the child of Elisabeth, now the great prophet of the wilderness, who was baptizing in the river Jordan.

'In those days came John the Baptist, preaching in the wilderness of Judea, and saying, Repent ye, for the Kingdom of Heaven is at hand.'

By 'the Kingdom of Heaven' he meant that restoration of the Theocracy, that promised reign of Messiah, that good time coming, of which all the prophets from Moses to Malachi had spoken; and to which the Jews were looking forward with an eagerness and a confidence that we can scarcely realize. By a careful calculation, based on Daniel's famous prophecy, they had found that the time was now fully come; that any day the Messiah might appear. Every text in their sacred books which spake of Him was diligently searched out, and repeated from mouth to mouth, that so they might be sure to recognise Him when He arrived. When they heard, therefore, that after a silence of four hundred years the spirit of prophecy had burst forth anew, that 'the word of the Lord' had come to John in the wilderness; when they found the Baptist clothed in the hair-cloth dress of the ancient prophets,—a man of the holiest, most ascetic life, content with such food as the desert afforded,—they made sure that it was He, the Messiah whom they were expecting. 'There went out unto him Jerusalem, and all Judea, and all the region about Jordan.' A deputation from the Sanhedrim waited on him, to know if it were so. But John denied that he was the Messiah; he was not the Messiah, but he was sent by God to announce His near approach. Whenever He, the greater One, should appear, John would be divinely enabled to recognise Him. This God had promised,—had promised him a sign from heaven, whereby he should surely know the true Messiah, and so be able to proclaim Him.

To the Baptist then Jesus came, undistinguished in the crowd. And yet as He approached John seems to have had a clear presentiment that it was He. Awe-struck and hesitating he baptized Him; anxiously looking for the promised sign. And the sign was given. As Jesus rose up out of the river, 'Lo, the heavens were opened unto him' (to John, but not to others, it would seem), 'and he saw the Spirit of God descending like a dove and lighting upon Him: and, lo, a voice from heaven, saying, This is my beloved Son, in whom I am well pleased.'

But it was not God's will that the Messiah should be at once proclaimed. The Spirit had withdrawn Jesus into the wilderness. Forty days He there spent in solitary communion with His Father, and in conflict with that Evil One, whose power over mankind He had come to break. Three times the Tempter assailed Him. Three times Christ repelled him, and each time by that 'sword of the Spirit which is the word of God :'—

'*It is written*, Man shall not live by bread alone, but by every word of God.' Thus Christ met the temptation of bodily appetite, of the *flesh*. No food, no care of ours, could sustain our bodily life a single day unless God so willed it : let us therefore do His will, and leave all else to Him.

Again, '*It is written*, Thou shalt worship the Lord thy God, and Him only shalt thou serve.' Thus He met the temptation to grasp at once the Messiah's dominion—the temptation of the *world*, as we may call it ; meaning that mere success is not a right aim or motive, but rather God's service.

And lastly, '*It is written*, Thou shalt not tempt the Lord thy God.' For the devil had bidden Him presume on God's providential care, fanatically. And between faith and fanaticism there is the widest difference : to trust that God will protect us while we are going His way, is faith ; to expect Him to protect us equally when going our own way, is fanaticism, called in Scripture a tempting of God. Unlike the temptations of the *flesh* and of the *world*, this last is a spiritual temptation, pride, a temptation of the *devil* peculiarly,—one that he reserves as his last snare for the saints of God.

Thus was the holy Jesus 'in all points tempted like as we are, yet without sin.' Thrice vanquished, 'the devil leaveth Him, and behold angels came and ministered to Him.'

Returning in the power of the Spirit to the banks of Jordan, where John was still baptizing, the Messiah was at once recognised by the Baptist ; 'there standeth One among you whom ye know not !' And again the next day, standing with two of his disciples, and looking upon Jesus as He walked, he saith, 'Behold the Lamb of God!' And the two, Andrew and the other one—unnamed, but clearly 'the disciple whom Jesus loved'—followed Jesus, and abode with Him that day.

They both seek Simon, and his brother Andrew is the first to find him, with the news, 'We have found the Messiah!' On the morrow the Lord himself bids Philip of Bethsaida join Him; and Philip findeth his friend Nathanael of Cana,—Bartholomew his other name,—all probably disciples of the Baptist.

Jesus and His five companions are invited—through Nathanael the invitation may have come—to a marriage feast at Cana. Our Lord's mother was already at the bridegroom's house; and *may* have been related to him, for we shall find her speaking as with authority to the servants. Joseph is no longer mentioned, and had probably long since been dead. Noticing that the arrival of the six new guests was causing some inconvenience, she turned to her Son, and called His attention to the lack of wine. Possibly it was the custom then, as now, in the East, for guests to bring their contributions to a feast; and Jesus had brought none. There was something in our Lord's reply which led Mary to expect that He intended by and bye to act on her suggestion, perhaps to send for wine[1], but not immediately. She therefore bade the servants do whatever He might tell them. Then Jesus turned to the six water-vessels —set probably for the customary washing of the six newly arrived guests after their journey—and bade the servants fill them with fresh water, and then draw and serve it to the chairman of the feast;

[1] Compare John xiii. 29.

and, behold, the water, as they served it, was changed into wine! The same divine power, which, by a slow process of secretion in the vine, turns the rain-drops into the juices of the grape, had wrought that self-same change instantaneously.[1] And thus did Jesus not only declare Himself the Lord of Nature, but also shadow forth, by way of emblem, the deep purpose for which He had come,—to change the natural life of man into a divine life, showing that 'the water that He would give should be a well of water springing up into everlasting life'.[2] In St. John's words, 'He manifested forth His glory, and His disciples believed on Him.'

They stayed not many days in Galilee. 'The Passover was at hand.' And at Capernaum they would find the caravan of pilgrims already gathering. And Jesus went up with the rest to Jerusalem.

And now that other distinct prophecy respecting the Messiah must be fulfilled :—'The Lord' must 'come suddenly to His temple, even the messenger of the covenant,' . . . 'and purify the sons of Levi.' Malachi's words may well have rushed into the minds of all, when He, whom the Baptist had so lately proclaimed as the Messiah, 'whose fan was in His hand, and who would throughly purge His floor,' appeared in the Temple, and with that scourge of small cords drove out the buyers and sellers and money-changers who were desecrating His Father's house. And when they asked Him by what authority He did these things, a yet greater sign than this He promised them,—in words misunderstood until the event explained them,

---

[1] See St. Augustine's admirable remarks on the 'Quotidiana miracula Dei,' in his 126th Sermon.
[2] John iv. 14.

—'Destroy this Temple, and in three days I will build it up,'—meaning the all-sufficient sign of His own resurrection. Thus distinctly, even from the first, was the end before Him, the great purpose of suffering for which He had come into the world.

Half convinced by His miracles at this festival, one of the Pharisees of high rank, Nicodemus by name, came to Jesus by night, afraid to confess Him openly, or join the baptized group on the banks of Jordan[1], but desiring to hear with his own ears a specimen of His teaching. Darkly, and under a figure which at the time Nicodemus failed to understand,—the figure of the *new birth*,—Jesus spake to him of that action of the Holy Spirit on the heart, which, begun in Baptism, must be more and more realized in the after-life of the Christian.

This was in April. The remainder of that summer and autumn Christ spent (St. John tells us) on the banks of Jordan, with those five disciples, baptizing His converts by their hands :—*He* ever increasing, John ever decreasing; the crowds that had followed John now following Jesus; and the Baptist rejoicing that it should be so.

Very affecting is this deep humility of the Baptist. Since the day when Moses stood on the further side of that same Jordan, surveying the promised land which *he* was not to enter, 'Tendebatque manus ripæ ulterioris amore'[2], there is nothing in history more affecting. The least in the kingdom of Christ's baptized was to be greater than he. His work was done; his end was drawing near. With the truest modesty, he combined, as all God's holiest servants have ever combined, the truest courage. In the power and spirit of

[1] Luke vii. 30.   [2] *Æneid* vi. 314.

Elijah he had rebuked the vices of Herod Antipas; and Herod cast him into prison, there to linger for nearly four months, and then to be sacrificed to the vengeance of the adulteress whom his rebukes had offended.

The imprisonment of the Baptist was near the close of the year. It was accepted by Jesus as a sign that the time was now fully come for a far more active and more public ministry; and He transferred His labours from the Jordan wilderness to the populous towns of Galilee.

His way lay through Samaria. St. John tells us how, resting by the way, He fell into conversation with the woman of Samaria, first about the divine life which all who would should draw from Him; and then, in reply to her controversial question, about the true worship of God, which henceforth was not to be confined to any chosen place or people, but was to be spiritual and therefore universal. 'God is Spirit: and they who worship Him must worship Him in spirit and in truth.'

After a two days' stay at Sychar,—a casual allusion dating it in January, for there wanted four months to the barley harvest[1],—Jesus passed on to Cana of Galilee, where, some nine or ten months before, He had made the water wine.

And here He worked His second wonder, healing by a word, and that too at a distance of five-and-twenty miles, the nobleman's son.

Thus we are brought to the end of St. John's fourth chapter, and to that point in the history at which the three earlier Gospels commence their account of the great Galilean ministry.

[1] John iv. 35.

CHAPTER III

Second Year, First Quarter

The great Galilean Ministry

THE whole period of our Lord's ministry, from His baptism to His crucifixion, according to the scheme of Irenæus[1], adopted in this narrative, covered two years and three months.

It may be conveniently divided into three equal portions :—

1*st*. The nine months spent in Judea previous to the imprisonment of the Baptist, embraced in the last chapter.

2*d*. The nine months spent mostly in Galilee, from the Baptist's imprisonment to the feast of Tabernacles in the October of the second year.

3*d*. The nine remaining months down to the last Passover when our Lord was crucified.

And of these three equal portions, the first and last (recorded mainly by St. John) were comparatively seasons of retirement.

The middle portion, on the contrary, on which we are now entering, was a season of incessant activity. Into it are crowded nearly all the miracles and most of the parables which fill the pages of the earlier Evangelists.

To arrange the numerous anecdotes of St. Matthew,

[1] Lib. ii. cap. xxii. 3. See Part III. chapter vi. of this volume.

St. Mark, and St. Luke, in their chronological order is (for reasons already given[1]) a difficult, perhaps an impossible, task. One point, however, breaking the nine months into two unequal portions of three and six, is fixed for us.

It is that memorable visit of our Lord to Jerusalem recorded in the fifth chapter of St. John. If, for reasons elsewhere[2] given, we reject Kepler's suggestion, and adhere to the more ancient opinion, that the festival there mentioned was the Passover, this visit must have been at the end of March (for the Passover fell on March 29 in this year), just after John the Baptist's martyrdom. So we have three months of Galilean ministry before, and six months of Galilean ministry after, this journey to Jerusalem.

On that earlier portion, on those three eventful months of January, February, and March, spent by our Lord in the crowded towns of Galilee, whilst the Baptist lay lingering in captivity, we now enter.

Thus much it seemed necessary to premise in order to clear up and justify the arrangement of this part of the narrative.

' The land of Zabulon and the land of Nephthalim, by the way of the sea, Galilee of the Gentiles—the people that sat in darkness saw great light! And to them which sat in the region and shadow of death light is sprung up!'

Galilee was the most northern and the most populous of the three provinces into which the Romans divided Palestine: a land of corn-fields, fisheries, and thriving towns; quite different from the sheep-walks and vineyards that hung upon the hill-sides of Judea. The effect of this difference in our Lord's teaching is.

[1] Part I. chap. ii.   [2] Part III. chap. vi.

very noticeable. In the Galilean parables of the three earlier Evangelists we are ever reminded of the seed-time and harvest, the fishermen and merchants, of that northern province; while in the Jerusalem discourses we hear rather of the flocks and the shepherds, the vine and the fig-tree of Judea.

Josephus[1] tells us there were more than 200 towns of Galilee, each containing on an average 15,000 people, no mere villages therefore, but large and thriving towns. The largest of them clustered on the western side of the Galilean lake—Capernaum, Bethsaida, Chorazin, Tiberias. This was the trading district, the Lancashire of Palestine; here the Romans had their custom-houses; here passed the great caravans which every Passover journeyed to the Holy City.

Gladly these Galileans seem to have welcomed their Messiah, when He came to take up His abode among them, after the imprisonment of the Baptist. Some remembered His miracle at Cana nine months before; many had witnessed His miracles at Jerusalem at the Passover, which they too had attended.

Quickly, therefore, would the news spread from town to town, that the mighty prophet had reappeared among them; and they of Capernaum could tell how on His first return to Cana He had healed by a word, at a distance of five-and-twenty miles, the nobleman's son (the son of Chuza and Joanna it may have been), who lay dying in their town.

One of the first places visited by Jesus in Galilee was Nazareth, His old home. In the synagogue, on the Sabbath-day, He stood up to read; and closing the book, declared that He had come to fulfil the prophecy they had just heard, that the year on which they were entering was the 'acceptable year,' that He him-

[1] *Bell. Jud.* iii. 3-20.

self was the Anointed One or Messiah, of whom Isaiah spoke. Awed at first by His divine eloquence, they listened and wondered; but when He began to speak of the far readier faith which He had found elsewhere, all their worst passions were roused; they thrust Him out; and had He not miraculously withdrawn Himself, they would have flung Him headlong down a precipice hard by.

Capernaum now became Christ's home. There He called upon His disciples, Andrew and Peter, James and John, to devote themselves more entirely than heretofore to His ministry. Others He added to their number: Philip doubtless, and Bartholomew, who had learned to know Him on the banks of Jordan; and, soon after, Matthew or Levi, one of the despised *publicans* or tax-gatherers in the Roman service.

His habit seems to have been to preach regularly in their synagogues on the Sabbath-days, being accepted as a Rabbi, even by those who questioned His Messiahship. Very striking is St. Luke's account of one of these early Sabbaths. Christ had been preaching with great power; and in the congregation there was a man possessed by the Evil One. Such possession was common in those days[1], especially among the fierce, undisciplined mountaineers of northern Galilee. It would seem as though it had been God's will that during the humiliation of His Son, the Evil One should be thus visibly brought face to face with Him who was to vanquish him. Here, as in the wilderness, the evil spirit at once recognised Jesus: ' Let us alone; I

[1] Others besides the New Testament writers testify the frequency of demoniacal possession. See Josephus, *Ant.* viii. 2. 5, *Bell. Jud.* vii. 6. 3, and Justin, *Apol.* ii. 6, both of whom mention cases of it as occurring at Rome.

C

know Thee who Thou art—the Holy One of God!' Startling must have been the effect on the bystanders of this immediate recognition; and still more startling the divine power of Jesus, when He silenced and expelled the demon before them all!

Returning to Simon Peter's house from the synagogue, and hearing that his wife's mother lay sick of a fever, He cured her by a word—so completely that she rose from her bed, and served to them their midday meal. And that same evening, so soon as sunset ended the Sabbath rest, we read how the excited crowd brought numbers to His door, some sick, some possessed by evil spirits; and laying His hands on them He healed them all.

Nor was His ministry confined to Capernaum. Touring through the towns of Galilee He 'healed all manner of disease among the people,'—among others the Leper, and on His return the palsied man whose sins the Lord forgave.

No wonder that after days of such incessant labour He was fain to withdraw into the solitudes of the hill-country, and there spend the night in prayer.

It was after such a night of prayer that He formally ordained the Twelve Apostles. All of them, not improbably, had been disciples of the Baptist; but since the close of the Baptist's ministry[1] they had one by one been called to follow Jesus. And now their number was completed, and on the second circuit through Galilee they were the attendants of their Lord. Some of them, as we have seen, were fishermen; and of their boats upon the lake Christ often availed Himself, when He wished to withdraw from the crowds who thronged Him, bidding them row Him across the lake to the less peopled valleys on the eastern side.

[1] Acts i. 21, 22.

It was in crossing the lake, after one of those days of long-continued preaching, that the storm overtook them which all three Evangelists have related. For convenience He had been preaching from one of their moored boats, while the multitude sat along the shore to listen. Over their heads, on the rising bank, He had seen, perhaps, 'the sower sowing his seed,' of whom in His parable He had been speaking, for it was still the early seed-time of the year. Exhausted as the evening drew on, Jesus asked them to unmoor the boat and cross the lake; 'and they took Him even as He was in the ship;' and Christ slept as they rowed, for seeing how weary He was, they had placed a pillow for Him in the poop. And there came down on the lake one of those sudden gusts of storm so common in mountainous countries; and the waves broke over the little ship. And they awoke Him, saying, 'Master, we perish!' Then He arose, and rebuked the wind, and the raging of the water, and there was a great calm. And they wondered, saying one to another, 'Who can this be? for He commandeth even the winds and water, and they obey Him!'

The next morning the stir of their landing, and of the crowd that came down to meet Him, attracted the attention of two miserable demoniacs, and they came running towards Him. Again Christ silenced and expelled the evil spirits; and in the horrid plunge of the maddened swine, into which the devils passed, all would see the hideously destructive nature of that Evil One from whom Christ came to redeem them.

But not only over the great enemy, not only over disease in every variety of form, but over the spirits of the dead also, Jesus asserted His divine power. Twice during this stay in Galilee we hear of our Lord recalling the dead to life. In the case of Jairus's daughter, the body's life was only that moment extinct; in the case of the widow's son at Nain, the corpse was being carried to the grave. In both that word of power summoned the spirit from the unseen world to return into the visible body. In both it was done in compassion for the bereaved parent, and to reveal Himself to His disciples as the Lord of life and death.

It was to these all-sufficient signs and credentials of Messiahship that Christ appealed, when from the Baptist in his captivity there came those messengers asking, 'Art Thou He that should come, or look we for another?' 'Go your way,' was Christ's reply, 'and tell John what things ye have seen and heard; how that the blind see, the lame walk, the lepers are cleansed, the deaf hear, the dead are raised, to the poor the gospel is preached. And blessed is he whosoever shall not be offended in Me.'

There is an undertone of sadness in these latter words that cannot escape us, contrasting as it does with the elation of the multitude around Him. While the Galilean peasantry were 'glorifying God, and saying that a great prophet was risen among them, and that God had visited His people,' Christ saw in this very enthusiasm how surely they would fall away from Him, as the real purpose of His mission began to be revealed. Gradually, as they could bear it, but more and more distinctly, He now began to declare unto them the spiritual nature of His kingdom.

How clearly is this the intention of that marvellous sermon on the Mount, which seems to belong to this period of the ministry!

How affectingly does He there set forth the meek, forgiving, lowly temper which must be theirs who seek admission into His kingdom! rejoicing when persecuted, returning good for the world's evil, ever looking, not to man, but to their Heavenly Father, for their reward ! How He unravels the secret motives of our conduct ! How He purges the conscience, and deep down in our consciousness of God lays the sure foundations of that Kingdom which, like a house founded on the rock, shall never fall !

Such was the new avenue to glory which Christ opened unto men ; an avenue of suffering and of self-abasement. But when He bade men follow He led the way Himself. Not only in His final passion, but all through His ministry, He bore our griefs and carried our sorrows. None can read these narratives attentively without perceiving it. There is something inexpressibly mournful in our Lord's sense of desolation, in the 11th chapter of St. Matthew, after His third circuit of Galilee. We see it in His lamentation over those cities 'wherein most of His mighty works were done,' 'because they repented not;'—in the bitterness with which He complained of their fickleness ; and still more in the plaintive close of the same chapter, where, turning from 'the wise and prudent' who rejected Him, to the childlike peasantry around Him, He bade them come to Him, all who laboured and were heavy laden, and He would give them rest :—' Take my yoke upon you, and learn of Me, for I am meek and lowly in heart ; and ye shall find rest unto your souls : for my yoke is easy, and my burden is light !'

Weakened by sorrow, exhausted by the pressure of the poor sufferers who thronged Him,—'for there were many coming and going,' and He had 'no leisure so much as to eat,'—dejected by the tidings of the Baptist's martyrdom, which had just reached Him, Jesus withdrew with His Apostles to the further side of the lake :—' Come ye yourselves,' He said, 'apart into a desert place, and rest awhile.'

CHAPTER IV

Second Year, Second Quarter

Passover and Northern Tour

HEARING of the Baptist's death, Jesus withdrew with the Twelve in their boat to a desert place across the lake to seek repose. But His repose was of short duration. The multitudes, already gathering for the approaching Passover, had seen His departure in the boat, and running round the head of the lake on foot, overtook Him on the green slopes of the north-eastern shore. And Jesus was moved with compassion, for they were as sheep having no shepherd, and had come from far with their wives and little ones, and were faint with hunger. So the Good Shepherd fed them wonderfully, five thousand of them, besides the women and children, out of that one basket, with its five loaves and two small fishes, and so abundantly that, when all were filled, the Twelve filled each his wallet[1] with the fragments that remained.

Gladly would the astonished multitude have carried Jesus in triumph to Jerusalem, and proclaimed Him their king. But Jesus withdrew into the hills, and bidding His Apostles row back across the lake without Him, spent the night in solitary prayer.

---

[1] Juvenal speaks of the wallet which every Jew carried, using the same word :—
'Judæis, quorum *cophinus* fœnumque supellex' (iii. 14).

A south-west gale had sprung up, and the disciples were still in the midst of the sea, trying in vain to make head against it, when, lo, between three and six o'clock in the morning, they saw Jesus walking on the sea, and making as though He would pass by them. But when they cried out in their fear, supposing they had seen some ghostly apparition, He spoke to them and said, 'Be of good cheer; it is I; be not afraid.' Then Peter, excited and raised by the sight of our Lord into that higher spiritual state in which one may well conceive the conditions of our bodily life may be suspended, stepped down upon the surface of the water, and went forward to meet Jesus—over-confident as ever! but the Lord sustained Him. And as Jesus entered the ship the wind ceased, and they found themselves at the further shore.

This miracle seems to have made a deeper impression on the Apostles than any previous one. 'They were sore amazed in themselves beyond measure, and wondered;' and another account says, 'They worshipped Him, and said, Of a truth Thou art the Son of God.'

St. John tells us how the next day in the synagogue at Capernaum Christ made this miracle of the loaves the text of His discourse. From the loaves which He had given them He endeavoured to raise their thoughts to the higher truth that He was Himself the bread that was given from heaven to be the sustenance of man's spiritual life; and for this He must be sacrificed, that they might feed upon the sacrifice, drawing all their nourishment from Him.

But this mystery was far too spiritual for their carnal minds—too deep even for His disciples. They thought to make Him their king, and He spoke of giving them His flesh to eat! What could He mean? And many turned away, and 'walked no more with Him.' Very touching is Christ's appeal to the Twelve, 'Will ye also go away?' and Peter's quick and earnest answer, 'Lord, to whom shall we go? Thou hast the words of eternal life. And we believe and are sure that Thou art the Christ, the Son of the living God.' And yet one of them (Christ said) was a traitor!

This was at Capernaum a few days before the Passover. We must now turn back to St. John's 5th chapter, for his account of this Passover[1].

'After this,' he says, 'was the[2] feast of the Jews, and Jesus went up to Jerusalem.' It was the Sabbath-day, the Paschal Sabbath, the greatest Sabbath of the year therefore; and Jesus had not only healed an impotent man at the Pool of Bethesda, but had bidden him rise and carry his bed. For this the man is charged before the Sanhedrim with Sabbath-breaking. He defends himself by saying that Jesus bade him do it; and Jesus therefore is Himself arraigned before them. This is the turning-point of the whole Gospel narrative. Ever since that purging of the Temple, twelve months ago, when they had sent their officers to ask 'by what authority He did these things,' the Pharisaic party had looked on Jesus with mingled fear and aversion,—fear because of His great popularity, aversion because of His unsparing denunciation of their hypocrisy. Now at last they have found their opportunity. This would-be Messiah is within their grasp: He is at their bar on the capital charge of Sabbath-breaking. And what is Christ's defence?

[1] For the order of events here adopted, see chapter vi. of Part III.
[2] The article is inserted in the Sinaitic MS.

The poor mendicant had sheltered himself under the name of his benefactor : to whom shall Christ appeal? Under whose name shall He seek shelter? Ah, blind malignant Pharisees, thinking to crush easily the Nazarene, were they prepared for Christ's appeal? Prophet of Nazareth no longer, leader of a Galilean multitude no longer, Christ stands before them as the eternal Son of Him whose Name they durst not utter!

Wonderfully does St. John in a single line sum up our Lord's sublime defence :—' My Father worketh hitherto, and I work !' 'The living God, whose energy upholds from day to day, from hour to hour, the work of His creation, He resteth not! nor yet can I, His Son! No Sabbath rest for me, until the work which He hath given Me be done! Not mine, but His the work : not Me, but Him are ye accusing ! to Him, the Holy One, My Father, I appeal.'

Not till He was gone, we may well believe, not till the majesty of that divine Presence had been withdrawn, did these impious men dare to pass their sentence against Him, not now for Sabbath-breaking only, but also for *blasphemy*. His words, His awful appeal, had not been misunderstood.

Jerusalem is now no safe place for Him : for He whose words thus quelled the most malignant, may lift no finger in His self-defence : and His hour is not yet come. Therefore at Jerusalem Christ must not stay except when filled (as during the feast-time) with His Galilean followers.

Abruptly He left Jerusalem, and returned to Capernaum. The one hope of the priestly party is now to set the Galilean multitude if possible against Him. Into Galilee their agents follow Him[1].

[1] Matt. xii. 2, xv. 1 ; Mark vii. 1. See Part III. chap. vi.

On the first Sabbath after the Passover[1] they find Him walking through the corn-fields, and allowing His disciples to pluck and rub the ears of corn. This is at once made an occasion for slandering Him as a Sabbath-breaker. Again, on another Sabbath in the Capernaum synagogue they are watching Him malignantly, whether He will heal the withered hand. How grandly St. Mark describes Him, looking round on them with anger, being grieved at the hardness of their hearts, and bidding the man stand forth, and healing him before them all! They were filled with madness, and went out and began to plot with the Herodian party, hoping through them, in all probability, to bring the Roman power to bear upon Him. But Christ at once withdraws, and the multitudes follow Him. '·Is not this the Son of David?' they cry; 'He maketh both the deaf to hear, and the dumb to speak.' 'Nay,' whispered the scribes, 'it is through the prince of the devils that He worketh these miracles.' Thus they blaspheme Him first as a Sabbath-breaker, and then as a demoniac. And now they have a third slander: 'Why do Thy disciples transgress the tradition of the elders? for they wash not their hands when they eat bread.' Severe and overwhelming was Christ's rejoinder, showing that it was *they*, not *He*, who transgressed; for defilement was from the heart, not from the hands. Let them beware whom they were resisting, not the Son of Man in His humiliation only—that might be forgiven if done in ignorance —but the Holy Spirit of God!

But thus far their malignity triumphed that to stay longer in Capernaum was impossible. It ceased to be

[1] See Part III. chap. vi. (pp. 138, 139), for the meaning of Luke vi. 1.

Christ's home. He went thence, we read (in the 15th of St. Matthew and the 7th of St. Mark), 'and departed into the coasts of Tyre and Sidon.'

It seems to have been for the purpose of seclusion rather than of preaching that our Lord retired to these distant regions. He was now beyond the extreme limits of the Holy Land, fifty miles north of Capernaum. The reading of our two oldest MSS.[1] makes it almost certain that He passed through the great Gentile town of Sidon, the most renowned seaport of the ancient world.

Even here the fame of His miracles had preceded Him, and, as St. Mark says, 'He could not be hid.' A poor mother, a descendant of the old Canaanite inhabitants of the land, came out of her house as He passed, doubting whether the great Israelite Healer would deign to notice her. 'Thou Son of King David,' she cried, 'my daughter is grievously vexed with a devil.' Jesus was silent, and was passing on. 'Send her away, for she crieth after us,' His disciples said. Jesus turned and spoke, 'I am not sent but unto the lost sheep of the house of Israel.' Then she came and fell at His feet, 'Lord, help me!' But He answered in the words of a proverb, 'It is not meet to take the children's bread and give it to our dogs.' 'Truth, Lord,' she replied, 'for the dogs are content with the crumbs which fall from their Master's table.' Christ's heart was so moved by the mother's prayers that He broke through the rule which He had laid down both

---

[1] Mark vii. 31. 'From the coasts of Tyre He came *through Sidon* unto the sea of Galilee.' The readings of our three oldest MSS. the unlearned reader may find in the Tauchnitz New Testament (Sampson Low, Son, and Marston, 2s. 6d.)

for Himself and for His Apostles[1]; and, though the hour of the Gentiles was not yet come, He granted her request; and thus showed forth to His disciples the mystery of the prevailing power of prayer.

It is not recorded that our Lord worked any other miracle during His sojourn in these parts, nor does it appear how long He stayed there. His mission was to the lost sheep of Israel, and to them He soon returned.

Through the half-Pagan population of the ten confederate towns lying to the east of the upper valley of the Jordan (called Decapolis), He journeyed back to the eastern shore of the Galilean lake, where a few weeks or months before He had fed the five thousand. And here once more a vast multitude gathered round Him. Three days they remained with Him, up among the hills; for it was now summer; days of incessant labour to Jesus. Group after group came before Him with their burdens of sick, casting them down at His feet. The lame, the blind, the dumb, the possessed, all were healed. And they glorified the God of Israel, and said of Jesus, 'He hath done all things well!'

It is noticeable that in the case of two of these miracles—the healing of a blind man's eyes with spittle, and a deaf man's ears at Bethsaida a few days later with finger-touch and spittle—our Lord seems to have found difficulty in the accomplishment of the cure, as though it was dependent in some measure on the degree of faith of the patient. The frequent phrase, 'Thy faith hath saved thee,' and on one occasion, 'He could do no miracle because of their unbelief,' confirms this explanation. They were a poor half-Gentile people on this eastern side of Jordan. Still they clung

[1] Matt. x. 5.

to Jesus, and there were no Scribes and Pharisees among them to poison their minds. And Christ was moved with compassion, and on the third day fed them once more—this time with seven loaves and a few little fishes—four thousand of them, besides women and children. And they took up seven baskets of the fragments after they had eaten.

CHAPTER V

Second Year, Third Quarter

Transfiguration and Feast of Tabernacles

ONCE during this sojourn in Decapolis our Lord crossed the lake to the Capernaum side, to see whether after His long absence they would receive Him. But no; the Pharisees, now leagued with the Sadducees, at once assailed Him, asking (as before) for the promised sign; and again Christ pointed to the great sign—darkly to them, under the emblem of Jonah, clearly to His Church ever after—the one all-sufficient sign of His resurrection from the dead.

Thus repulsed, our Lord seems to have re-embarked forthwith in the vessel by which He came, and returned to the further side to Bethsaida Julias. From thence He bent His steps northward once more, this time up the Jordan valley to Cæsarea, a highland town, and favourite resort in the summer heat, much beautified of late by the tetrarch Philip, lying at the foot of the snow-capped Hermon, at the very source of the Jordan.

It was 'by the way,' as they journeyed up the valley, that that remarkable conversation took place between our Lord and His Apostles, in which He sought to prepare them for His approaching sufferings, and also for that glimpse of the promised glory to which those sufferings were to lead.

He had been questioning them about the people's opinion of His own divine Person, and had drawn forth from Peter the good confession, 'Thou art the Son of the living God,'—a confession which Christ rewarded by the promise that Peter should be one of the foundation-stones of His Church, with power to grant or refuse admission thereinto. Content with this, He forbade them to make Him further known (doubtless fearing lest any outburst of Galilean enthusiasm should hasten the end prematurely); and then began to declare to them far more clearly than heretofore the sufferings that awaited Him,—that He must go to Jerusalem, fall into the hands of the Sanhedrim, be put to death, and be raised again the third day.

Not without much inward conflict had Christ prepared Himself to drink this cup of suffering. In Peter's reply, 'Be it far from Thee!' He seemed to recognise the whispering of one who more than once (it may be believed) had tempted Him to grasp the Messiah's kingdom *without suffering;* hence the repulse of the suggestion as though it came from the Tempter himself, 'Get thee behind me, Satan.' And in the exhortation to His disciples to sacrifice all, even their lives, if need be, for God's sake, we see that this was the one thought now uppermost in His mind, the thought of sacrifice,—that only by suffering could He 'enter into His glory,' and so fulfil all that 'Moses and the Prophets had written concerning Himself'[1].

Then He added a distinct and emphatic promise that the glory of His kingdom should be revealed to some—not to all, but to some—of those present, very shortly.

To three of them, only a week later—as all three

[1] Luke xxiv. 26.

Evangelists are careful to tell us, clearly connecting what followed with this conversation—was vouchsafed a foretaste of that glory, more wonderful, more impressive, more convincing, than anything they had yet witnessed. He had taken Peter, James, and John apart from the rest, and led them up into a high mountain to spend the night in prayer. And as Jesus prayed a great change was seen to come over Him,—'His face did shine as the sun, and His raiment was white as the light.' The three Apostles were heavy with sleep, but they were awakened by the dazzling light, and kept awake throughout the vision (διαγρηγορήσαντες εἶδον): and, behold, there talked with Him two men which were Moses and Elijah, who appeared in glory, and spake of His decease which He should accomplish at Jerusalem. 'They spake of His decease,' and so bore witness, the one for the Law and the other for the Prophets, that it was a suffering Messiah to whom both Law and Prophets had ever pointed.

And as the two seemed to be departing Peter would fain have detained them; but just then there came the luminous cloud, or Shechinah, the emblem of Jehovah's presence, and overshadowed them; and the Apostles feared as they saw the three enter into the cloud, and fell on their face, and were sore afraid, and heard a voice as it were out of the cloud, 'This is My beloved Son: hear Him!' And as they lay on the ground Jesus came and touched them, and said, 'Arise, be not afraid;' and they looked up and found themselves once more alone with Jesus.

As they came down from the mountain He charged them, saying, 'Tell the vision to no man, until the Son of Man be risen from the dead.' And they kept that saying within themselves, questioning what the rising from the dead, of which Christ had thrice so lately spoken, should mean.

Such was this mysterious revelation, vouchsafed to three Apostles, for their own sakes exclusively (as appears from this charge of secrecy) until the yet greater sign should come. How deep an impression it left upon them, we know from the way in which one of them alludes to it in his old age, near forty years afterwards[1].

Some trace of the dazzling glory seems to have lingered on Christ's countenance, as on that of Moses when he too came down from the mount; for St. Mark tells us that 'all the people when they beheld Him were greatly amazed.'

His holy presence might well shame the scene of strife and tumult in the valley. The nine Apostles had failed to cast out an evil spirit ;—on one side were Christ's old enemies the Scribes, pointing triumphantly at the disciples' failure ; on the other the unhappy father, vainly imploring their assistance ; in the midst the evil spirit himself, still in possession of his victim, and maddened by the sight of the Holy One who approached. Here too faith seemed necessary to the cure,—faith not of the dumb helpless child, but of the father answering in the child's behalf. Feeble was his faith, more of the heart than of the head ; but Christ accepted it, expelled the demon, and with His own hand raised the fainting boy from the ground.

So passed the summer months, from April to September.

After the Transfiguration Our Lord returned to Capernaum[2], giving His Apostles for the second time

[1] 2 Pet. i. 16-18.
[2] At Capernaum, from the anecdote of the collection of

a distinct prediction of His Betrayal, Death, and Resurrection. There His brethren, as they are called —His half-brothers probably,—came to Him and urged Him to accompany them to Jerusalem in the great caravan of pilgrims then forming for the Feast of Tabernacles[1]. Though they believed not on Him, still they were proud of His miraculous powers, and wished Him to display them at Jerusalem. But the time for finally transferring His ministry from Galilee into Judea was not yet come. Our Lord declined to join the caravan, and delaying His journey some few days, travelled up privately with few if any of His apostles, and not till the festival week was half over went publicly into the Temple to teach.

The appearance of the now famous Galilean Teacher in the Temple caused no small stir among the Jews. They wondered how He could have acquired so much Scripture learning, not having been the pupil of any of their great Rabbis. His courage too in thus showing Himself publicly surprised them. For since His cure of the impotent man on the Sabbath-day at the previous Passover, their rulers had proscribed Him as a Sabbath-breaker and blasphemer; and for six months He had absented Himself from Jerusalem. 'Is not this He whom they seek to put to death?' they said, 'but, lo, He speaketh boldly, and they say nothing

the Temple tax—the half-shekel levied on all *householders*, in the autumn of each year,—we may infer that Christ had still a home, where possibly Mary, and perhaps His half-brothers, made their abode.

[1] It seems strange that any should identify these 'brethren' with any of the Apostles, when St. John adds so plainly— 'For neither did His brethren believe on Him;' and St. Luke (Acts i. 14) mentions them so distinctly *in addition to* the Eleven. See Prof. Lightfoot's exhaustive essay in his 'Galatians.'

unto Him. Have our rulers discovered that He is after all the Messiah?' Boldly our Lord defended that Sabbath miracle; and on the last great day of the Feast, when the water from Siloam was brought in procession and poured on the high altar, He claimed it as a type of that Holy Spirit which He would Himself pour forth upon mankind. The priests dared not touch Him. Jerusalem was much too full of Christ's Galilean followers at these great festivals to allow of His apprehension. Even the officers whom the Sanhedrim sent to seize Him, came back into the council-chamber, saying, 'Never man spake like this man:' and one even of their own number—the same Nicodemus, who, eighteen months before, had sought by night an interview with Jesus—ventured to remonstrate with them on His behalf. But in vain; 'was He not a Galilean? and could the Messiah come from Galilee?'

So ended the Feast of Tabernacles. When Jesus next appeared in the Temple we shall find the priests taunting Him, not with His Galilean origin, but with being a *Samaritan.* This was something new, and requires explanation. And the explanation is supplied, I believe, by St. Luke's Gospel, to which we now turn.

CHAPTER VI

Second Year, Fourth Quarter

Final Return to Judea, and Feast of Dedication

ALL the three earlier Gospels tell us distinctly and emphatically how, not long after His Transfiguration, our Lord with His twelve Apostles bade farewell to those Galilean cities where He had so long sojourned, and set forth on His final public progress towards Jerusalem. Clearly this could not be that journey to the Feast of Tabernacles, for then St. John tells us Christ travelled 'not openly, but as it were in secret.' We must suppose, therefore, that after the Feast of Tabernacles—after the close, therefore, of St. John's 7th chapter (where by some mistake the beautiful anecdote of the woman taken in adultery has got inserted)—our Lord, privately, as He had come, left Jerusalem, and rejoined His Apostles at Capernaum, and there commenced His preparations for this solemn Messianic progress towards the scene of His approaching sufferings. To St. Luke, as I have said, we owe our knowledge of this striking journey.

Never before, so far as it appears, had Christ taken His twelve Apostles with Him to Jerusalem. Now He not only takes them, but, rallying round Him a great multitude of His followers, He places Himself at their head, and 'steadfastly set His face to go to Jerusalem.' Nor is this all. He sends messengers before His face to prepare the Samaritans to receive

Him, for through Samaria He means to travel—Chorazin, Bethsaida, Capernaum, had rejected Him. To the Samaritans,—yes, to the despised Samaritans He will now appeal. To the Twelve, in his earlier ministry, He had said, 'Into any city of the Samaritans enter ye not!' Not so to the Seventy evangelists whom He now sends forth, Into those fields of Samaria, which, ten months before, He had seen already whitening unto the harvest, He will now send forth His labourers. In His parable of the Good Samaritan, He reproves the exclusive prejudices of His Jewish followers; among the lepers whom He cleansed in the border country, He is careful to point out that the only thankful one was a Samaritan. Thus He journeys on from village to village; gathering followers as He goes. His last pause is at Bethany, where those faithful friends, of whom we now for the first time hear, Martha and Mary, receive Him, Martha serving, and Mary choosing the better part—the one thing needful,—and sitting at His feet.

But Christ, thus brought to the very gates of Jerusalem, will not now make His triumphal entry. It is December, and more than three months are yet wanting to the Paschal season, and not till the Paschal season can Christ our Passover be slain. Therefore, after a brief sojourn in the neighbourhood of Jerusalem—perhaps at Bethany,—Christ purposes to draw off His followers to the more secluded banks of the Jordan, and there resume awhile that ministry in the wilderness, which, just a year ago, He had discontinued[1].

[1] We may observe, in passing, how exactly the accounts of St. Matthew (xix.) and St. Mark (x.) agree here with St. John. Both of them imply a pause between this public journey up

For Christ's brief sojourn in or near Jerusalem, and for His public teaching in the Temple in this month of December, we must turn to the 8th, 9th, and 10th chapters of St. John. In the 8th chapter, we find our Lord in the most public court of the Temple, called the Treasury, proclaiming Himself, as Isaiah and holy Simeon had proclaimed Him, not merely the Messiah of Israel, but a Light to lighten the Gentiles also, 'The Light of the whole World.'

Never before had Christ so fully declared Himself in Jerusalem. When they quote against Him His own words, spoken eight months before, that if He bore witness of Himself His witness would not be true, He vindicates Himself by appealing to the perfect union between the Son and the Father. In this twofold witness the maxim of their law was fulfilled.

The calm majesty of His words seems again and again to abash them. When they venture to ask, 'Who art Thou?' He replies, 'When ye shall have lifted up your Messiah from the earth, then shall ye know that I am He.' 'Then shall ye, too, who believe on Me, be redeemed from your slavery, and be made the sons of God.'

The multitude is still divided, some standing by Christ, others angrily resenting this imputation of being slaves. *They* slaves, forsooth! they, of the pure blood of Abraham, *slaves!* and this from a Samaritan, for as such they now revile Him: 'Say we not well, that Thou art a Samaritan, and hast a devil?' (Possibly some of this despised race, who had

from Galilee and the triumphal entry into Jerusalem on Palm Sunday. Both tell us that this interval was spent in the confines of Judea beyond Jordan.

joined Him in His progress through Samaria, were seen with Him in the Temple.)

Their brutal taunts only draw forth from Jesus more and more clearly the declaration of His own divine eternal nature. They can bear it no longer. They will stone the blasphemer on the spot. But His disciples close around Him, and our Lord is enabled to withdraw Himself from their violence.

It was on the following Sabbath, and again in the streets of Jerusalem, that our Lord, wishing to show forth the divine truth that He was the Light of the World, gave sight to a poor blind mendicant. Very touching is the courage and faith of this poor man, when summoned to the bar of the Sanhedrim for this breach of the Sabbath. Boldly avowing his conviction that Jesus is from God, he is excommunicated as a heretic. Our Lord finds the outcast, and reveals Himself yet more fully to him as the Son of God.

Then, turning to the blind Pharisees, He denounces them as false shepherds, and proclaims Himself to be the good shepherd who giveth His life for the sheep. St. John is careful to tell us how great was the effect of our Lord's words. Not only the multitude, but many, even of the hostile party, bore witness to their power.

Thus Jerusalem was divided: some crying, 'He hath a devil, and is mad: why hear ye Him?' others saying, 'These are not the words of one who hath a devil. Can a demon open the eyes of the blind?'

Once more before He withdraws to the further side of Jordan Christ will deliver His testimony in the temple. It was the Feast of Dedication,—answering almost exactly to our Christmas,—and our Lord was in the cloister called Solomon's Porch. Again He declared His divinity: 'I and my Father are one!' And again they took up stones to stone Him for what they deemed His blasphemy,—'because that Thou, being a man, makest Thyself God.' And Jesus is compelled to quit Jerusalem, not to appear again in her sin-stained streets until the final Passover. On the banks of Jordan He rejoined the multitude of His disciples, Galileans mostly, and followers of the Baptist of old. But here was One far greater than the Baptist, 'For John did no miracle; but all things that John spake of this man were true.' Here Christ stayed among them, healing their sick and teaching; and thus the winter months went by[1].

And here we pause. We have had before us Christ in the Temple at the Feast of Tabernacles, then that solemn public progress up from Galilee through Samaria into the confines of Judea; and lastly we have had those December discourses in the Temple, in which our Lord bore such unreserved witness to His own divinity. As the end approached our Lord can more and more afford (if one may so speak) to cast off that reserve with which in His earlier ministry He had shrouded His own divine nature. Well He knew that precisely in proportion as He revealed His own divinity, in that same proportion would the hate of these malignant Jews be deepened, and the end be hastened. There is nothing in human record so tragical, nothing so terrible, as St. John's description in these latter chapters of the ever deepening hatred with which these Pharisees thirsted for the blood of that Holy One who had appeared among them. His words, His very presence, testified against them that their works and hearts were evil.

[1] Matt. xix. 2; Mark x. 1.

CHAPTER VII

Third Year, First Quarter

𝕽aising of 𝕷azarus and final 𝕬scent to 𝕵erusalem

WE have now reached the last three months of our Lord's ministry, the first three months of the thirty-third year (humanly speaking) of our Lord's age—the January, February, and March of our calendar. Our Lord has withdrawn (as we have seen) from Jerusalem, and has gathered a vast multitude of His disciples around Him beyond Jordan, where John at first baptized. There He ministers to them, healing their sick and teaching. Possibly to this period of His ministry belong those 15th and 16th chapters of St. Luke, so rich in parables,—the parable of the Lost Sheep, of the Prodigal Son, of the Unjust Steward, of the Rich Man and Lazarus. From that retirement once, and once only, so far as appears, was He drawn away into the neighbourhood of Jerusalem. We have seen how on His great journey from Galilee into Judea His last resting-place was Bethany, in the house of those two sisters, Martha and Mary,—the house of Simon the leper it is elsewhere called. Possibly Simon was the father, or possibly the husband, of Martha, but being leprous was in seclusion, or possibly he was dead, but the house was still known by his name. However that may be, there Martha and Mary and Lazarus lived, and Martha was mistress of the house; and there Jesus had often found a quiet resting-place when Jerusalem was unsafe for Him.

A message from these faithful friends is brought to Him in His retirement beyond Jordan, brief and sad, from the two sisters, 'Lord, behold, he whom Thou lovest is sick.' Brief, and yet enough. Well those sisters knew Christ's love for their brother Lazarus. Well they knew, too, His almighty healing power. Christ was some thirty miles off, yet not much further than He had been at Cana when with a word He healed the nobleman's son at Capernaum. Yes! a word would have sufficed in answer to their prayer. But Christ had other purposes in view, unknown to Martha and Mary. For the greater glory of God He will yet delay. Two days He lingers beyond Jordan, two days are spent upon the journey. On the fourth day He draws near to the village. Anxiously they had been expecting Him. They had received His message, so mysterious, clearly intended to keep alive their hope, and yet ere it reached them their brother was no more.

First Martha and then Mary go forth to meet the Lord. How full of pathos—sorrow mingling with confidence in Christ's love—and what a seeking for sympathy there is in their simple greeting, 'Lord, if thou hadst been here our brother had not died.' By a few words of profoundest meaning Christ seeks to lift them into that higher point of view in which what we call death ceases to be death; and that higher life He connects mysteriously with His own person—'I am the resurrection and the life!'—meaning that death is no interruption to the life in Christ. Their brother is still living, though beyond the veil; and this He purposes to prove to them by calling him back into his mortal body. But meantime their natural grief moves Him deeply; they bring Him weeping to the grave. Many mourners stand around; at His bidding they remove the stone that closed the entrance. Again by an effort restraining His emotion, He lifted up His eyes and said, 'Father, I thank Thee that Thou hast heard Me. And I knew that Thou hearest Me always; but because of the people that stand by I said it, that they may believe that Thou hast sent Me!' And when He had thus spoken He cried with a loud voice, 'Lazarus, come forth!' Then from the recesses of the tomb, moving with difficulty, bandaged hand and foot with grave-clothes, and a napkin over the face, the quickened corpse came forth. 'Loose him, and let him go!' And Lazarus stood by his sisters' side! Such was this sign, this mightiest sign of His divinity that Jesus had thus far shown on earth: proving Himself to be Lord both of living and of dead. One only greater sign He showed, a few weeks later, when by His divine life He reawakened His own body.

During the few remaining days of Christ's ministry Lazarus appears to have been His companion. When next he visited his sisters' home it was as their guest, newly arrived with our Lord from Ephraim.

The miracle, as Jesus doubtless foresaw, was followed by the most important consequences; on the one hand it convinced many even among the hostile party that He was the Messiah, and so swelled the number of His adherents in Jerusalem that except by treachery it was now impossible for the rulers to seize Him. On the other hand His enemies saw plainly that further to delay their murderous purpose was most unsafe. A meeting of the Sanhedrim was called at once. Alarmed and perplexed, they expected that the Galileans might now any moment rise with Jesus at their head, and march against the Roman garrison at Jerusalem, and that the Romans would make the insurrection an excuse for enslaving—perhaps destroying—their city and nation. Little did Caiaphas know the deep prophetic truth that he was uttering when he told them it was expedient 'that one man should die for the people.'

It was decreed, therefore, that come what might Jesus should be sacrificed—should be handed over to the Roman executioner, although he were one of their own blood, rather than provoke further the jealousy of their oppressors. Thus they cloaked their own personal malice under a show of policy, and gave orders that if any man knew where Jesus was he should inform them.

Meanwhile our blessed Lord had withdrawn from Bethany to a town called Ephraim, near to the wilderness, not far, perhaps, from Jericho; there, out of reach of His enemies, He seems to have awaited the approach of the Galilean caravan of pilgrims to the Passover.

On the 7th of Nisan (Thursday), followed by His Apostles and a multitude of Galilean disciples, our Lord once more set forth on the highway that led through Jericho to Jerusalem—to Jerusalem, where, as they knew, a hundred enemies thirsted for His blood! Something there seems to have been in His outward demeanour—He leading the way, and they following behind—that filled His disciples with awe and amazement. 'And as they followed,' St. Mark tells us, 'they were afraid.' And Jesus took the Twelve apart, and said unto them, 'Behold, we go up to Jerusalem;

and the Son of Man shall be betrayed unto the chief priests, and unto the scribes, and they shall condemn Him to death, and shall deliver Him to the Gentiles (*i.e.*, to the Romans), to mock, and to scourge, and to crucify; and the third day He shall rise again.' But St. Luke adds, 'And they understood none of these things, and this saying was hid from them, neither knew they the things that were spoken.' For still they dreamed of a temporal kingdom, and still their only thought was who should have the highest rank therein!

Near Jericho, the crowd ever increasing, He gave sight to blind Bartimeus, and lodged for the night at the house of Zaccheus, chief among the excisemen of the town. Heretofore Zaccheus had served Mammon, henceforth he will serve God: for the words of his divine guest have touched his heart, and he vows that he will give half his wealth to the poor, and restore fourfold whatever he has wrongfully exacted. Partly, no doubt, in connexion with this act of faithful stewardship, and partly, as St. Luke tells us, to correct their notion that the Messiah's kingdom in glory was to be established immediately at Jerusalem, Christ spoke the parable of the Pounds, signifying that not now, but at His second coming, after His 'long journey,' would His kingdom of glory appear, and that in the meantime His servants must be faithful stewards of the gifts of grace bequeathed to them.

Again He set forth on the morrow, on the Friday or Preparation-day, Himself as before leading the way, ever ascending to Jerusalem. That evening—St. John is careful to fix the day, 'six days before the Passover' —He rested at Bethany, and there spent the Sabbath. It was at the house of Simon the leper, the house of

Martha and Mary, at their Sabbath meal, while Martha served, but 'Lazarus was one of them that sat at the table with Jesus,' that Mary came with her costly perfume and anointed her dear Lord. Very refreshing in that climate is such fragrant lotion, a thousandfold more precious to our Lord was the devoted love which inspired the act, connected as it was in our Lord's mind, and possibly in Mary's, with His approaching death.

Meantime the news had reached Jerusalem that the Messiah was within a mile and a half of its walls. That evening, so soon as the Sabbath rest was over, 'much people of the Jews came, not for Jesus' sake only, but that they might see Lazarus also, whom He had raised from the dead.'[1]

[1] Why do the three earlier Evangelists not even mention this most stupendous of Christ's miracles? The following answer has been suggested. They wrote in the lifetime of Martha, Mary, and Lazarus. Well might one about whom there hung the mystery of having passed through death desire privacy. Nay, his own personal safety required it; for we read that the Sanhedrim sought his life, 'because that by reason of him many of the Jews went away and believed on Jesus.'

Not, therefore, till that generation had passed away was the miracle published. The last of the Apostles, writing sixty years or more after the event, far away at Ephesus, records with all the vividness of an eye-witness what had sunk deep into the memory of all the Twelve. So, too, and doubtless for like reason, he alone of the Evangelists publishes the name of him who came to Jesus by night, and brought spices to His tomb.

CHAPTER VIII

Early Days of Holy Week

'TELL ye the daughter of Zion, Behold, thy King cometh unto thee, meek, and sitting upon an ass, and a colt the foal of an ass.' So was it written in the Prophets, and so must it be fulfilled by Christ. Every act and every word is now full of deepest meaning. The ass 'and the colt with her' are duly found and brought. Seating the spare form of their divine Master on the foal, they leave the wooded dell of Bethany, and slowly ascend the rocky path which leads over the shoulder of the hill towards Jerusalem. Thousands of Galilean pilgrims follow in His train. A vast multitude from the Holy City stream forth to meet them, tearing down the long vernal fronds of the palms, and waving them with loud Hosannas as they approach. Eagerly they tell or hear of all the wonders He has done, —and most of all of Lazarus. Is not this the Messiah, their promised king? Nor shall royal honours be wanting: the crowd that meet them, turning and heading the procession, strew the path with their palm-leaves, while others carpet the ground under His feet with their garments. Thus the long procession sweeps over the crest of the hill, and the Holy City bursts upon their view. Again the Messianic psalm is raised by the disciples, ' Blessed be the King that cometh in the name of the Lord; peace in heaven and glory in the highest!' And the multitude in front take up the strain, while they that follow make answer, waking the echoes of the deep ravine with their Hosannas. Nor does He, the Messiah, refuse their adoration; 'I tell you, if these should hold their peace, the stones would immediately cry out.'

But another vision was rising before the prophetic eye of Jesus; a vision of Roman armies, of long lines of siege, of ruin, and of slaughter; and as He gazed at the beautiful city, He wept over it, saying, 'If thou hadst known, even thou, at least in this thy day, the things which belong unto thy peace! but now they are hid from thine eyes.'

Again they move on, slowly down through the olive-gardens, and across the deep torrent bed of the Kedron, and up the rocky slope on the further side, and so through one of the city gates to the levelled ledge of Mount Moriah, on which the Temple stood. The whole day, the whole of that Palm Sunday, seems to have been spent in this solemn entry[1].

St. Mark simply tells us that Jesus entered the Temple; 'and when He had looked round about upon all things, and now the eventide was come, He went out again to Bethany with the twelve.' Early, as it would seem, on Monday morning, Jesus again bent His steps towards Jerusalem. Hungering by the way, He went up to a fig-tree, whose unusually early show of leaves made Him expect to find fruit; but finding none, and following the train of feeling with which the sight of the city on this same spot the day before had filled His mind, He spoke His thought aloud, and said, 'No man eat fruit of thee hereafter

[1] No one who has read it can forget Dean Stanley's vivid description of this Entry, in his *Sinai and Palestine*.

for ever!'—oh that His people had shown the fruit that He looked for in this day of His visitation! But now it was *too late!* Passing on He entered the Temple. Once more shall 'the Lord come suddenly to His temple, and purify the sons of Levi.' As at the first, so now at the last, Passover of His ministry, He purged the holy courts of His Father's house of the unseemly traffic which profaned them. The multitude crowd around Him, bringing their blind and their lame: and the Messiah heals them all. The chief priests and scribes can bear it no longer; for the very children were crying, 'Hosanna to the son of David!' 'Hearest Thou what these say?' they ask indignantly. 'Yes,' Christ answers; 'have ye never read, Out of the mouth of babes and sucklings Thou hast perfected praise?' In the present temper of the people it was impossible to lay hands on Him. The day was spent in the Temple; in the evening He withdrew again to that favoured home at Bethany.

Tuesday, the 12th of Nisan, appears to have been spent from early dawn to near sunset in the Temple in public teaching. In their early morning walk across the Mount of Olives, the disciples noticed that the fig-tree was already withered,—such was the power of even the least of Christ's words! And such too might be the power of *their* words (He told them) if only they would pray in faith.

In the Temple, which He had cleared the day before, He was met by a deputation from the Sanhedrim, asking by what authority He had done it. Christ silenced them by asking in return, in the hearing of all the people, to what authority they ascribed the reformation which the Baptist had preached—divine or human? They could not for shame say St. John's mission was divine, for they had themselves rejected him; they dared not say it was human, for all the people believed in him. Thus either way they would be discredited in the eyes of the multitude. Then Christ took up His parable against the Pharisees, and denounced their hypocrisy before all the people. They were like the son who said unto his father, 'I go, sir,' and went not; they were like the wicked husbandman who slew the Heir when He came to seek fruit from His vineyard; they were like the rebellious guests who refused to come to the wedding feast. Even such were these Pharisees, and even thus were they drawing down on themselves that fearful retribution which so continually, during this week, rose up before Christ's vision.

Stung to the quick by these parables, His enemies would there and then have laid their hands upon Jesus; but the people protected Him, and their baffled rulers retired to their council-chamber to concert another mode of attack. Their only hope now was to discredit Him either with the Romans on one side, or with the populace on the other. They will frame a double-edged question, which He cannot answer without giving offence either to Pilate or to the Jews: and that His answer, on whichever side it be, may be duly witnessed and reported, they send, along with the Pharisees, some Herodians—courtiers of the Roman power. With flattering words they pretend to be referring to Him a case of conscience. 'What thinkest Thou, is it lawful to give tribute to Cæsar or not?' Little were they prepared for the divine simplicity with which our Lord at once evaded the snare, rebuked their malice, and proclaimed one of the great principles of His kingdom. 'Why tempt ye Me, ye hypocrites? show me the tribute-money.' 'Whose is this image and superscription?' Thus He obliged them with their own mouth to confess the master whom, for their sins, God had placed over them. 'Render, therefore, unto Cæsar the things that are Cæsar's, and unto God the things that are God's.' Thus Christ reconciled for ever the duty of obedience to *human law* and to *divine law*,—whatever hardship we suffer under the first, must be accepted as a penalty for our disobedience to the second. Assuredly as we obey the second, so surely will God's providence bring about an amendment of the first.

One party in the Sanhedrim being thus foiled and silenced, another party came forward. The Sadducees believed not in a future state, and thought they would perplex Jesus on this much-disputed question. They put the case of a woman who had seven husbands in this world, flippantly asking ' whose wife shall she be in the next?' Not content with showing the folly of their question—all such relationships ceasing in the other world,—Christ proved from their own Pentateuch the doctrine they denied. Jehovah would not continue to call Himself the God of Abraham, Isaac, and Jacob, unless Abraham, Isaac, and Jacob were still living ! He is not the God of the dead, but of the living : for all live unto Him !

One more among their number—a lawyer—made a last attempt to draw Him into controversy, asking which was the greatest of the commandments ; but seems to have been so struck by the wisdom of Christ's answer, that he was almost induced to range himself on His side.

Thus one and all they stood discomfited. And now it was their turn to be questioned. As in His reply about the resurrection, so now in His question about His own divinity, our Lord declared a truth of the very deepest import to His Church in all ages, while to those about Him He seemed to be but engaging in one of those discussions about the letter of Scripture of which alone their narrow minds were capable. 'Whose son do you expect your Messiah to be?' They answer, 'The son of David.' 'How then is it that David in the 110th Psalm is inspired to call Him Lord?' Thus did Christ show them that in failing to recognise His divinity they failed to understand their own Scriptures.

But this kind of victory in argument was far from being what Christ most cared for. His chief concern was to guard His flock from being corrupted morally by this Pharisaic party. Sternly He now reproves their evil lives and practices, their cruelty, their hypocrisy, their pride: and fearful are the woes that He denounces upon them. And as the vision of the coming doom once more rises before Him, His voice—as of one exhausted by strong emotion—sinks into tones of mournful tenderness:—'O Jerusalem, Jerusalem, thou that killest the prophets, and stonest them that are sent unto thee, how often would I have gathered thy children together, even as a hen gathereth her chickens under her wings, and ye would not! Behold, your house is left unto you desolate. For I say unto you, Ye shall not see Me henceforth, till ye shall say, Blessed is He that cometh in the name of the Lord.' And so He left the Temple courts.

But our record of this eventful day is not yet closed. Pausing, perhaps while the crowd dispersed, in the chamber where stood the chests for the people's Temple-offerings, our blessed Lord, Whose eye is ever on the lowliest, noticed a poor widow casting in her two mites. And he called unto Him His disciples, and said unto them, 'Verily I say unto you, that this poor widow hath cast more in than all they that have cast into the treasury: for all they did cast in of their abundance, but she of her want did cast in all that she had, even all her living.'

As they left the Temple, the disciples called our Lord's attention to the marvellous masonry of the wall which overhung the ravine; but this too our Lord assured them would be laid in ruins in the coming doom. Resting on the slope of Olivet, they asked Him when all this should be, and what would be the sign of His second coming, and of the end of the world. Then with the dark shadow of the Temple in the foreground and the sinking glory of the sunset beyond, our Saviour revealed so much as He was permitted to reveal of those 'times and seasons which the Father hath put in His own power.'

It is plain from the disciples' question that they took it for granted that the fall of Jerusalem would be the end of the world. Our Lord is careful to correct this notion: 'Let no man deceive you; Jerusalem must be trodden down by the Gentiles, and that too in the lifetime of this generation; but the end is not yet; the times of the Gentiles must first be fulfilled.'

How long 'the times of the Gentiles'—this interval between the fall of Jerusalem and the end of the world—would be, whether months, or years, or centuries should intervene, was left purposely unrevealed. Enough that the disciples, when that which most nearly concerned them came to be fulfilled, and the Roman armies gathered round the holy city, understood the signs of their Lord's warning, and saved themselves from the impending woe. God grant that we too, whenever the end of all shall draw near, may also read aright the signs of the latter portion of this prophecy; and be among those 'faithful servants' found watching for their Master's coming, among those 'wise virgins' whose lamps will then be trimmed and burning!

Of Wednesday the 13th of Nisan we have no very certain record,—unless we assign to this day St. John's anecdote of the Greek proselytes, who, not venturing themselves beyond the outer court of the Temple, sent within to Jesus desiring an interview[1].

As when Nicodemus, two years before, came to Him in the Paschal week, seeking a specimen of His divine teaching, so now to these Greek strangers our Lord vouchsafed one of those weighty sayings in which a deep truth lay half revealed: 'Verily, verily, I say unto you, Except a corn of wheat fall into the ground, and die, it abideth alone; but if it die, it bringeth forth much fruit.' The decay of the earthly is necessary to the growth of the heavenly. And yet how painful is this decay of the earthly—painful to all, a thousand-fold most painful to Him who felt as none other has felt its connexion with the sin of the world! And as He thought thereon a spasm of the approaching agony seems to have passed over the soul of Jesus; when, lo! there came, for the third time since His baptism, that mysterious sustaining voice from heaven; and some thought it thundered, and some that an angel spake to Him. But to Jesus

[1] There seems no reason why we should suppose that our Lord discontinued on this day what St. Luke tells us was His *daily* practice during this week, of repairing early each morning to the Temple. On Tuesday, as we have seen, the multitude were still decidedly in His favour; on the Friday we know how they had fallen off from Him. St. John's narrative supplies the signs of this gradual defection which the interval seems to require.

the crisis was for the moment over; and He began to speak freely of His own death and the manner of it, and how in so dying He should draw all men unto Himself.

But this death of the Messiah was precisely what the multitude could not and would not accept. They had always understood that Messiah was to live for ever; how could He be lifted up on the cross? If so, then He was not the Messiah they were expecting! Thus darkened and blinded by their sins, even as Isaiah had foretold (and this is St. John's only explanation of their conduct when he reflects thereon), these very men who but a day or two before had filled the air with their Hosannas, now rejected their Messiah when He spake of His crucifixion. With a few solemn words of warning Christ withdrew from the Temple, and this time, as St. John tells us, was compelled to hide Himself from them.

The week began with triumphant songs and loud Hosannas. Two days of bitter controversy between Christ and the Pharisees followed. So far the Galilean multitude were still with Him. But on the fourth day their loyalty, as we have seen, began to waver. Sternly Christ refused for the sake of their support to compromise in the very least degree those spiritual purposes for which alone He came into the world. And they fall away from Him; the very men whom He had fed on the shore of the Galilean lake, whose sick He had healed, who had followed Him to Jerusalem, who had strewn His path with their garments,—fall away from Him:—

'Hosanna now, to-morrow Crucify!
The changeful burden still of their rude lawless cry!'

CHAPTER IX

The Last Supper and the Betrayal

TO understand aright the four accounts of our blessed Lord's last Supper and Betrayal, we must bear in mind the order of the Paschal feast, and mark well the notes of time which the Evangelists give us.

The Jewish day was a night and a day, extending from sunset to sunset. On the afternoon of the 14th of Nisan the Jews used carefully to put away all leaven from their houses; and before sunset,—before the close of the 14th therefore,—each household sacrificed its Paschal lamb. After sunset (at the beginning therefore of the 15th Nisan according to their reckoning) the lamb was roasted, and the feast of the Passover began, lasting all through the night. The whole lamb was to be consumed in the course of the night, though not necessarily at one meal. It was eaten with the unleavened bread and wine, and sweet sauce and bitter herbs. This was the Lord's Passover, commencing at the close of the 14th Nisan, and lasting through the night.

We take up our narrative on the afternoon of Thursday, our Lord sending Peter and John to the house of an unnamed disciple—unnamed perhaps for fear of bringing him into trouble—to prepare their Paschal meal.

There in the upper chamber, when the hour was come, our Lord and His twelve Apostles assembled to celebrate their last Passover together. Long they remembered,—as long as they lived,—the solemnity of that leave-taking; remembered how He, the Son of God, full of His own deep thoughts, knowing that He was come from God and was going to God, had poured shame on their want of humility by kneeling down Himself to wash their feet.

And they needed the lesson. Strange and almost incredible it seems, that, even at this last supper, they were disputing (as St. Luke tells us) about precedence. Humility, therefore, was the first lesson that Christ would teach them. But there was another more mysterious lesson which our Lord desired on this last evening to impress deeply on their mind, and, through them, on the mind of His Church for ever—and that was the doctrine of His own sacrifice.

Many times He had spoken to them of His approaching death as a sacrifice,—a sacrifice of which in some transcendent way His people were to be partakers. But they had failed to understand Him. This deep truth, therefore, that they and we were to draw all our spiritual nourishment from His sacrificed body and from His poured-out blood, He will now show forth and fix in a sacramental act that His Church may repeat 'in remembrance of Him' through all time, to her great and endless comfort.

Not only does our Lord bind His Apostles together into communion one with another, by dividing among them the loaf that was before Him, and bidding all pledge themselves in the one cup; but, more than this, He binds them also into a mysterious communion with Himself—for He calls that bread His Body, and that wine His Blood. Yes, this was His deeper meaning, not bread and wine, but His own Body, His own Blood was in His thought—this it was that He was giving for the life of the world. None can draw life from the Holy Communion unless he feed therein, in heart and mind, upon the Sacrifice of Christ. Does any ask what is meant by feeding on Christ? Our Lord's discourse at this last supper is recorded by St. John on purpose to explain it. The purpose of that discourse from first to last was to prepare His disciples to understand that He was not forsaking them, but only changing His outward and visible presence into an inward, invisible, and far more effectual presence. He left them outwardly that He might return to them inwardly. Whoever receives Him thus inwardly returning, the same feeds on Him; and never so effectually as in the Holy Communion of the Lord's Supper.

The 17th chapter of St. John gives us our Lord's prayer, as He lifted up His eyes to the moonlight sky on their way to Gethsemane, and prayed aloud for them, and added, ' Neither pray I for these alone, but for them also who shall believe on Me through their word; that they all may be one, as Thou, Father, art in Me, and I in Thee, that they also may be one in Us!' Such were the far-reaching thoughts of love that filled the mind of Christ on this night, up to the very hour of His agony. It is well to notice this; up to the very last, up to the very entrance into the garden, so far as we may gather from that 17th of St. John, our Lord's mind was serene and tranquil, full of the joy of returning to His Father's glory, full of the yet deeper joy of sharing that glory with those whom He was redeeming. But not without sacrifice, not without draining to the last drop this cup of anguish, can He redeem them. He knew it: and the hour had now come. Scarcely had He kneeled in the garden when the agony came upon Him—dark, crushing, for the moment overwhelming, as if the sorrows of hell were upon His soul. Bowed and falling forward to the earth, it seemed as though His Father had forsaken Him, as though the Evil One was permitted in this hour of darkness to overshadow Him, permitted to make trial of Him to the very uttermost. It is terrible; can none share the travail of His soul? None! Can none even watch with Him? None! Alone He must tread the wine-press! 'I looked and there was none to help, and I wondered that there was none to uphold.' But with strong crying and tears He sent up His prayer unto Him that was able to save Him from fainting utterly, and was heard, and an angel was seen to be strengthening Him in His exhaustion. How fearful this struggle with the Evil One had been, the Apostles knew when they saw the crimson stains of perspiration where He had knelt. But it was over. Calm and tranquil, as before, was now again His voice, as He approached them, 'Sleep on now, and take your rest: it is enough.'

An hour or more this agony must have lasted, for thrice He came and woke the three Apostles, whose eyes were heavy with sorrow and the lateness of the hour, and twice they again had fallen asleep. The third time He told them it was too late now to watch with Him. The traitor was at hand. And immediately, while He yet spake, came Judas to the entrance of the garden; and with him an armed band of Jewish and Roman soldiers, with torches and lanterns. 'Jesus, therefore, knowing all things that should come upon Him, went forth, and said unto them, Whom seek ye?' Then followed the preconcerted kiss of the traitor, the recoil of the men from that holy presence, the care of Jesus for His disciples' safety, Peter's attempted resistance, and Christ's reproof, asking permission of the soldiers who held Him to heal the servant whom the rash sword-stroke had so nearly slain. Could He, whose merest whisper would have given Him twelve legions of angels, need the sword of man to defend Him? It was His Father's will, and therefore *His* will that He should suffer all. So the soldiers bound Him, and led Him away. Then the Apostles, and that other disciple who seems to have risen hastily from his bed on hearing the alarm, forsook Him and fled.

The priests, who accompanied the soldiers, directed them to take Him to the palace of Annas, who, though no longer high priest, seems to have retained the chief power. The actual high priest was Caiaphas, his son-in-law, who occupied, perhaps, a portion of the same palace. Having met with no resistance, they had brought their prisoner sooner than the priests expected, and some hours must elapse before the Sanhedrim could be assembled. The interval was spent in a private examination of Jesus by Annas, interrupted only by the brutal servant who struck Jesus in the face to force Him to reply.

Meantime the Apostle John, who was known to the high priest, had gained entrance to the palace, and had asked the damsel who kept the gate to admit Peter also. As Peter passed her she said, 'Art thou not one of His disciples?' Peter denied it. Again mingling with the servants round their fire in the court-yard, and still hoping to escape notice, he was charged by the same maid, or by another, with being a disciple. Again he denied it. Meantime the day was breaking, and the Sanhedrim was assembling in the chamber of Caiaphas. Thither now Annas sent his prisoner. It was perhaps in crossing the courtyard that one of the High-Priest's slaves in charge of Jesus, a kinsman of the Malchus whom Peter had wounded, recognised the Apostle as one of those whom he had seen with Jesus in the garden; others too now joined in the taunt; and a third time Peter denied his Lord, and immediately the cock crew; and Jesus turned and looked upon Peter. And Peter remembered the word of the Lord, how He said to Him, 'Before the cock crow, thou shalt deny Me thrice.' And he went out and wept bitterly.

CHAPTER X

Judgment in the Jewish Court

IN the last chapter we had before us the events of the Thursday evening of Passion Week. The Paschal Supper, the Agony, the Betrayal, and Peter's denial, filled up the hours of that night from sunset to cock-crowing, that is, till three o'clock.

We now enter on the events of Good Friday. So full are our sacred records of this day, so momentous each of its details, that we must divide our narrative into three portions : two will describe the trials of our Lord, and the third the crucifixion.

And first the two trials, if trials they may be called, must occupy us. It is important to keep them distinct : one trial in the Jewish court before sunrise, and the other trial in the Roman court after sunrise. These early hours were nothing strange in those times and countries ; Roman magistrates not unusually administered justice soon after sunrise. And, besides, we may remember what a strong motive the Jewish rulers had for getting the business finished as early as possible. Beyond all things they feared an uproar among the people. This Friday was the greatest feast-day in the year. In the forenoon there would be the great Temple sacrifice, followed by the feast. They must have all over before the forenoon if possible.

Therefore the Sanhedrim had been summoned to meet at the first breaking of the day, at five o'clock or thereabouts,—not in the Temple, that would have been hardly legal before sunrise, but in the house of Caiaphas. The false witnesses were in readiness. The priests made sure of being able to convict Jesus of blasphemy. Any attempt, however, to carry out their sentence by stoning Him on the spot, according to the law of Moses (Deut. xii.), would be highly dangerous, and sure to offend the Romans, who reserved to themselves the exclusive right of inflicting capital punishment in all their conquered provinces. The policy of the Pharisees, therefore, was first to procure a condemnation in their own court on the charge of blasphemy, and then to carry the case into the Roman court, expecting that the procurator, Pontius Pilate, would, as a matter of course, execute their sentence. And if the sentence were to be executed by Romans, then it must be, not by stoning, but by crucifixion; for so did the Romans put to death criminals who had not the rights of citizenship. This, then, was their plan of proceeding; and thus did these evil men bring about the fulfilment of all that Christ had foretold concerning the order of the Passion:—'The Son of Man shall be betrayed unto the chief priests, and unto the scribes, and they shall condemn Him to death; and shall deliver Him to the Gentiles, to mock, and to scourge, and to crucify; and the third day He shall rise again.' Thus in most exact detail had our Lord predicted all that was to befall Him. He was first to be betrayed to the priestly party; secondly, to be condemned in the Jewish court; thirdly, to be delivered over to the Gentile, *i.e.* to the Roman power; fourthly, to be mocked, scourged, and crucified. We have seen already how the betrayal took place under cover of the night, while all the Galilean pilgrims were indoors eating their Passover. We are now to see how the condemnation, first in the Jewish, and then in the Roman court, and then the Roman mode of execution, with the preliminary scourging, were all brought about in Divine Providence as the hours of Good Friday went by.

And first the condemnation in the Jewish court.

The morning light had scarcely streaked the sky above the mountains of Moab, when the Sanhedrim met, and Jesus, who had been kept waiting in the chamber of Annas, was taken across the court-yard to the hall of Caiaphas, and there placed at the bar of the Sanhedrim.

But in this first stage of the proceeding their evidence broke down. 'For many bare false witness against Him, but their witness agreed not together.' Then came two men who remembered what Christ had said at the Passover feast two years before, and thought by a slight perversion of the words to turn it into blasphemy against the Holy Place : 'We heard Him say, I will destroy this temple that is made with hands, and within three days I will build another made without hands. But neither so did their witness agree together,' for on cross examination doubtless the truth came out that Christ had said 'Destroy,' not 'I will destroy.'

Then the high priest, following the custom of the court when evidence failed, put the prisoner upon His oath :—'I adjure Thee by the living God that Thou tell us whether Thou be the Messiah, the Son of the Blessed.'

Observe, not the Messiah merely—for to have

claimed Messiahship would not have been so certainly a blasphemy,—but 'the Son of the Blessed,' that higher title which Jesus was understood to have claimed, and which no mere man could claim without fearful blasphemy. If they could only force Jesus to repeat this claim in open court, His condemnation and death would be certain.

One can imagine how hushed the court would be while the high priest put the question ; how all eyes would be turned on the mysterious Person at the bar ; how breathless the attention when He who had been hitherto silent accepted the oath, and slowly and distinctly affirmed that He was what the high priest said, —the Messiah, the Son of the Blessed ; adding that henceforth they should see Him,—their Messiah, the 'Son of Man' of Daniel's prophecy,—standing on the right hand of God.

One more chance they gave Him—their malignity could well afford it—say rather God's Providence chose thus to foreclose for ever any doubt His Church might else have had,—one more chance they gave Him to explain if haply He did not mean all that those words seemed to imply: 'Art Thou, then,' many voices asked, 'the Son of God?' And He said unto them, '*I am*.' Then the high priest, rising from his seat, and rending his linen tunic from the neck downwards, after the manner of the Jews when they heard what their religion abhorred, put the question to the court : 'He hath spoken blasphemy, what need we any further witness? Ye have heard the blasphemy, what think ye?' And the verdict came by acclamation, 'He is guilty of death.' Then Jesus seems to have been removed from the hall and exposed to the brutal mockery of the attendants, while the Sanhedrim adjourned to the Temple[1] and deliberated how best they might now insure the execution of their sentence[2]; and it was agreed to take the case at once before the Procurator, while it was yet early, and before the day's sacrifice should draw together the crowd of Paschal worshippers. So Jesus was again chained[3] by the wrist to the Roman soldiers,—for St. John implies that a detachment of the Roman cohort had been placed at the Sanhedrim's service,—and was taken by them to Herod's palace on the Western Hill, which the Roman Governor used as his Pretorium during all these great festivals, his residence at other times being at Cæsarea, on the coast.

[1] There Judas found them (Matt. xxvii. 3, 5).
[2] Matt. xxvii. 1.   [3] Matt. xxvii. 2.

CHAPTER XI

Judgment in the Roman Court

THE chief priests and other leading members of the Sanhedrim followed their Prisoner as far as the Pretorian gate, but went not into the Gentiles' hall, lest they should be defiled. So Pilate came out to the deputation, and, seeing Jesus bound, asked what accusation they brought against Him. The Jews answered that if He were not a malefactor they would not have brought Him; that it was a case for capital punishment, which their court, as Pilate knew, had no power to inflict. They expected that Pilate would be willing to oblige them, and simply execute their sentence. But this Pilate would not do, requiring some specific charge of which his own court could take cognisance. So the Jews, well knowing that Pilate would neither heed nor understand their charge of *blasphemy*, brought forward a new charge against Jesus—the charge of *treason*, treason against the Roman empire: Jesus, they said, had affected to be a king, stirring up the people to insurrection, and forbidding to pay tribute to the Roman emperor. Then Pilate went back into the house, and summoned the Prisoner before him. Thus the second trial before the Roman magistrate began, for the account of which we are mainly indebted to St. John.

Writing, as St. John did, for a later generation,

when the Temple and the Jewish polity were swept away, and the Roman Empire was all in all, we need not wonder that to him this second trial, in which the divine Author of Christianity and the representative of the Roman Empire were brought face to face, had come to be more interesting than that first trial in the Jewish court, on which the three earlier Evangelists as naturally dwell.

Deeply interesting, too, to the modern student, is the dialogue that now ensued between the Redeemer of the world and the highly educated Roman knight. Not only were the two principles of Church and State confronted, but also Christianity and this world's philosophy were to try conclusions.

In the bad, worldly man before whom He stood, Jesus recognised merely the official instrument of Divine Providence. Not to him, but to the Jews, belonged the chief sin of these proceedings; therefore to Pilate's half-sarcastic, half-curious questions, Christ answered, with reserve indeed, but with sufficient clearness to make it plain that between the divine kingdom which He was founding, and the kingdoms of this world, there never was, nor ever could be, aught of rivalry or competition. One only right Christ claimed for Himself and for His kingdom, the right of 'bearing witness to the truth.'

Freedom of speech, liberty to persuade all who are willing to be persuaded, this is all that Christ asked, all that His Church may ask, as of divine right, at the hand of the State. Nor needs she more. They who are of the truth will hear her voice. Christ wants no other subjects for His kingdom.

All this to Pilate seemed the merest, the most harmless enthusiasm. He went out to the Sanhedrists and said, 'I find no fault in Him.' They persisted that He had been a teacher of sedition all over the country, first in Galilee, then in Jerusalem. Hearing mention of Galilee, Pilate gladly seized the pretext for dismissing the case from his jurisdiction to that of the Galilean tetrarch, not sorry thus to gratify a native prince whom he had recently offended. To Herod Antipas, therefore, who was in Jerusalem for the feast, he sent them with their prisoner.

This sensual superstitious tyrant had often wished to witness some of Christ's miracles; and he asked Him many questions. Offended by His silence, he set Him at naught with his body-guard; and sent Him back to Pilate in one of his cast-off robes.

Then Pilate again addressed the members of the Sanhedrim, saying, that neither he nor yet Herod had found Him guilty of any political crime. But they were louder than ever in their accusations, for the day was drawing on, and a crowd was beginning to assemble. Pilate, now perceiving plainly that the priests and scribes were actuated in the main by jealousy of Christ's popularity, thought he might perhaps gain something by an appeal to the people. It was his custom at these great festivals to gratify the populace by releasing some political prisoner. Pilate proposed, therefore, by way of compromise, to allow the usual preliminary of a Roman execution, the scourging by the lictors, to take place, and then to release Jesus. But while the wooden tribunal, a sort of pulpit, was being brought and placed on the tessellated pavement in front of the palace, ready for the judgment, the priests were busy among the crowd persuading and exciting them to ask rather for the release of Barabbas, who for a murderous plot against the Roman power had been sentenced to death. Pilate's sending into the house for the tribunal made his wife aware that judgment was going to be pronounced, and scarcely had he taken his seat when a message came from her entreating him to have nothing to do with that Just One, for in the sleep from which she was just awakening dreams about Him had troubled her.

More anxious than ever, Pilate asked the people which they would have him release, 'Jesus or Barabbas?' And they cried, 'Barabbas!' 'What, then, must I do with Jesus, your Messiah?' They shouted, 'Crucify Him, crucify Him!' Again Pilate appealed to them, 'Why, what evil hath He done?' But the voices of the scribes and of the priests prevailed that Jesus should be crucified.

In vain Pilate protested; in vain he appealed in dumb show to the crowd beyond, washing his hands before them all, according to the Jewish custom, and saying, 'I am guiltless of this man's blood,' 'see ye to it.' 'His blood be on us, and on our children!' they madly cried. Thus again was the irresolute Pilate foiled. Thinking it just possible that if the proposed scourging were carried into effect they might then relent, he gave orders that it should be done.

Then did the Holy One 'give His back to the smiters, and His cheeks to them that did pluck off the hair, and hid not His face from shame and spitting.'

For we read that the savage soldiery in the courtyard, not content with the lictors' scourging—terrible as a Roman scourging was,—arrayed Him again in the crimson robe, and put a mock crown of thorns upon His brow, and a reed for sceptre in His hand, and making their approaches and obeisances as unto a king, struck His face with the palms of their hands, and spat upon Him, buffeting Him.

'But He was wounded for our transgressions, He was bruised for our iniquities : the chastisement of our peace was upon Him ; and with His stripes we are healed.'

Again Pilate came forward, and pointing to Jesus said, 'Behold the man !'—as much as to say, 'Is not this enough to content you?' But still they clamoured for crucifixion. 'Take ye Him, and crucify Him!' Pilate said ironically, knowing they had no power to do it, 'for I find no fault in Him.' Then the priests, seeing that their charge of treason had so utterly failed, fell back upon His condemnation in their own court for blasphemy. 'We have a law,' they said, ' and by our law He ought to die, because He made himself the Son of God ;'—showing again how clear and unmistakable had been Christ's claim to be all that we believe.

These words seem to have increased the superstitious fears which his wife's dream had awakened in Pilate ; and again he withdrew to question Jesus within as to His origin. But this time Jesus was silent. Before, when Pilate had questioned Him as a magistrate on a charge of treason, our Lord answered him ; but now, when Pilate questions Him from curiosity, He is silent.

'He was oppressed and He was afflicted, yet He opened not His mouth. Who shall declare His generation ? For the transgression of God's people must He be stricken.'

Our Lord's silence, and the calm dignity of His reproof when Pilate sought to threaten Him, disturbed and perplexed Pilate more than ever. But whatever scruples he had were scattered to the winds by the cry which assailed him when he again came forth to the excited crowd. The threat of being informed against at Rome for conniving at sedition, was a threat before which many a better Roman viceroy had quailed. Such a whisper in the ears of his jealous master was the very thing that Pilate dreaded, the very thing which six years later led to his disgrace and ruin.

He yielded at once, and, mounting the tribunal, gave sentence for the execution of the Prisoner.

CHAPTER XII

The Crucifixion

WE have now reviewed in memory all that happened in the earlier hours of Good Friday :—the trial before the Sanhedrim preceding sunrise, and the trial before Pontius Pilate occupying apparently the first hour of the daylight. I say 'apparently,' for there is a difficulty about the exact time, which must strike all who carefully compare these Gospels. St. John dates very emphatically (xix. 14) the conclusion of that later trial, that moment when Pilate mounted his tribunal and gave his final order for the crucifixion. 'It was the Passover Friday,' St. John tells us, '*and about the sixth hour.*' Now St. Mark tells us no less emphatically, and no less clearly, that the moment of erecting the cross was *the third hour*. How are these two dates of time to be reconciled ? By the third hour St. Mark necessarily means what we call nine o'clock in the morning. If St. John adopts the common Jewish reckoning, his phrase 'the sixth hour' would mean twelve o'clock, and this could not possibly be reconciled with the account of the three other Evangelists. It is conjectured therefore that St. John, writing far away for the Churches of Asia Minor, adopted another mode of reckoning like our own, and by the sixth hour meant what we call six o'clock, not long after sunrise[1].

At this point, then, when Pilate gave the final order for the execution, between six and seven A.M., we take up our mournful narrative.

Had Jesus been a Roman citizen, as St. Paul was, His head would have been struck off by the lictors who had scourged Him. But being an alien, His sentence was the sentence of a slave, that he should be impaled on a cross along with two felons who had also been condemned to death. A centurion's guard would now be told off to carry the sentence into effect. Our Lord's upper garment was restored to Him; and the three prisoners, each carrying the cross-piece of wood to which the hands were to be nailed, were conducted to the place of execution. This was just outside the city walls, that is certain; probably it was where Constantine's Golden Gate now stands, on the very verge of Mount Moriah, where it overhangs the valley of Kedron[2]. From Herod's palace on the Western Hill down the steps—those steps on which Paul stood to address the crowd,—along the terrace, over the bridge (the remains of which were discovered the other day), and then across the northern part of the

---

[1] The argument in favour of this conjecture may be found in Dr. Townson's learned dissertation. If it be adopted nearly all difficulty is cleared away. Pilate gave judgment 'about' six o'clock, some time, that is, between six and seven; and we have more than two hours left for the procession to Golgotha and the preparations for the Crucifixion.

[2] This question we may hope to have settled by the excavations now going on. The fields outside the Horse Gate, just to the north of the Temple, were not inclosed within the city walls until A.D. 45. In Jeremiah's time it was a place of 'dead bodies' (Jer. xxxi. 40); Athaliah was executed there (2 Kings xi. 16).

Temple hill through the Horse Gate to Golgotha, would be three-fourths of a mile. Weakened by loss of blood, for a Roman scourging was very severe, our Lord seems to have been unable to proceed with His burden, for we read that the soldiers at the city gate transferred it to the shoulders of one Simon a Cyrenian, whom they met coming in from the country, and pressed into their service. It is interesting to know that this man's sons, and probably himself too, became Christian converts.

It was probably during this pause on the way of tears—pictured for all time by the greatest of Christian painters; those who know not the picture will remember the engraving, Raphael's 'Spasimo,' as it is called,—the Redeemer, crushed beneath His cross, turned to the wailing women who followed Him, and, with the thought of the impending judgment once more rising in His mind, bade them weep not for Him, but rather for themselves and for their children, for the days were coming when they would pray that yonder hill of Olivet might fall upon them and bury them—for if such were the beginning of sorrows what would the end be?

Arrived on the ground, the guard would be formed into an open square round the prisoners, to keep off the crowd, while four of their number were charged with the task of crucifixion. The clothes were taken off, and formed the perquisite of the four soldiers; hence the dividing of our Lord's outer garment—the large square shawl or *bernouse* still worn in the East —into four parts; and the casting lots for the long seamless Galilean shirt. 'They parted My garments among them, and for My vesture did they cast lots.'

Two of the soldiers held each a hand, and one the

feet, while the fourth drove in the nails, the body resting on a short projecting bar. Then the cross, being nine or ten feet in length, was slowly reared with its sacred burden. The soldiers, or perhaps the centurion, offered Jesus a stupefying draught; but the first taste told what it was, and Jesus refused to drink it. The cup which His Father had given Him, *that* He would drain in all its bitterness. Over His head was nailed Pilate's inscription, written in Greek, Latin, and Hebrew, so as to be understood by all: 'Jesus the Nazarene, King of the Jews,'—Pilate's sarcasm bearing witness to the fulfilment of all prophecy.

The thieves were also crucified, one on either hand. Thus did the soldiers ruthlessly fulfil their orders. 'Father, forgive them; they know not what they do!' these were the only words that escaped the lips of Him whom they were crucifying.

It was now nine o'clock; six hours remain of lingering agony. His mother and her sister (who seems from the parallel accounts in St. Matthew and St. Mark to be Salome), with Mary the wife of Cleopas or Alphæus, and Mary of Magdala, stood by the cross, and with them the disciple whom Jesus loved, the only one of the Apostles who shared the women's holy courage. Doubtless the nearest friends would be admitted by the centurion within the square. Jesus, seeing His widowed mother, commended her very solemnly to the care of St. John, who forthwith, apparently, took her to his home in the city—himself returning in time to witness later the piercing of the side. The other three seem to have withdrawn to the further side of the narrow Kedron valley, for St. Matthew and St. Mark mention them by name as standing, at a later hour, amongst those who were looking on 'afar off.' Indeed, to remain near the cross would now be hardly safe for the women. The soldiers, their work done, had been withdrawn, leaving only the centurion and the four, who remained under arms to see that no rescue was attempted. The Scribes and Pharisees could now freely approach, and ceased not to blaspheme Him with the priests. 'Thou that destroyest the Temple and buildest it in three days, save Thyself!' 'If Thou be the Son of God, come down from the cross.' 'He saved others, Himself He cannot save!' 'King of Israel, indeed! let Him come down from His cross and we will believe Him!' 'He trusted in God, let God now deliver Him if He will; for He said, I am the Son of God!'

Thus have we an accumulation of evidence, witness on witness, that Jesus had been clearly and unmistakably understood by all who were present at the trial —not disciples, but enemies—to claim that divinity, that share in His Father's throne, which the Church has ever ascribed to Him.

But holier and yet deeper evidence than this is ours: even the evidence on which our faith must ever mainly rest—the power of Christ's Spirit over the heart of man. Never was Christ's quickening energy so manifest as when, in this hour of extreme suffering, He put it forth to redeem the dying sinner at His side. While one thief was hopelessly hardened, with the other it was not so; and Christ saw it. And to the softened humbled heart of the miserable man Christ turned, and so filled it with His grace that there came forth that prayer of faith—when the faith of all around was failing,—'Lord, remember me when Thou comest into Thy kingdom!' And the blessed, oh ! the infinitely blessed, answer was his, 'This day shalt thou be with Me in Paradise.'

Nor could the powers of Nature withhold their witness to Him by Whose word they were created. From twelve to three o'clock, we read, there was darkness,—no eclipse, for the moon was at the full,—there was a preternatural darkness over all the land, followed by an earthquake. We hear no more of the scoffs of the priests and scribes during that mysterious gloom.

Four times only was the silence broken by the words of Him Whose spirit was in agony: the first cry, 'Eli, Eli, lama sabachthani !' 'My God, my God, why hast Thou forsaken me ?'—which the soldiers, half understanding the Chaldee, mistook for a crying for Elias. And then, as the inward fever increased, 'I thirst.' And when one, softened by the sight, amid the jeers of his comrades, lifted the spongeful of sour wine to His parched lips, that cry of deepest meaning, 'It is finished !' And once again a last loud cry, 'Father, into Thy hands I commend My spirit !' It was the last; the breathing had ceased; the sacred head had sunk upon the breast.

CHAPTER XIII

The Burial and Resurrection

GOOD FRIDAY'S sun was sinking where we left off in our narrative—sinking, but not set; an hour or two remained of daylight, and something we have yet to tell of that remaining time, and of the Sabbath-day that followed, ere we come to the Easter morning.

The gloom, the deep darkness, which had hung like a pall over the land, was clearing away; the earthquake had been felt by many: and the yawning graves which it had opened were connected afterwards in the disciples' minds with the apparitions of departed friends, to which several bore witness after the Lord's resurrection. But at the time, thoughts of the passing hour, as ever, occupied them :—the soldiers of the watch thinking only of their routine of duty; the Jews—those blinded Jews—thinking only of the letter of that law, whose divine Author they had crucified, lest the dead or dying bodies, if left hanging after sunset, should pollute their Sabbath-day, and therefore urging Pilate to make sure of their death and have them taken down. In the two thieves life was still lingering; their death must therefore be hastened by a blow of the club. In the sacred body of our Lord life they found extinct; and the Scripture is fulfilled,

'A bone of Him shall not be broken.' But one of the soldiers, to make sure, thrust his spear into His side, and forthwith came thereout after the spear blood and water. And thus the other Scripture was fulfilled, 'They shall look on Him whom they pierced.' And thus, too, was the Apostle St. John, who had returned and was standing by the cross, enabled to silence for ever those who in his later days denied the *reality* of Christ's body and Christ's death.

And now must God's Providence—ere yet Good Friday's sun have fully set—prepare for that yet greater sign which is to follow.

The body of the Holy One must not be thrown into the undistinguished grave of those two thieves. No: God will prepare a chamber which itself too shall bear its witness. Therefore was Joseph of Arimathea moved to venture into Pilate's presence with the bold request that the body might be given to him for burial; and therefore was the sepulchre a new one, 'wherein was never man yet laid.' The witness of that vault on Easter-day must be complete, not one body less than before, but *empty*. 'A good man and a just' was this Joseph; and though a member of the Sanhedrim, he 'had not consented to their counsel and their deed.' And with him came, too, that other faithful member of the Sanhedrim—not now by night, but openly,—the wealthy Nicodemus, with his costly offering, a hundred pounds weight of myrrh and fragrant aloes-wood. Gladly from the hands of the rude soldiers they receive the bleeding body: and with reverent care in Joseph's garden, which was near the spot, they lay it down, and swathe it in their linen clothes, putting their powdered perfumes between the folds. There is not time to anoint the body, nor was stain of embalming to be upon Him Who was to rise. But the two Maries are sitting there, beholding all; and will return so soon as the Sabbath rest shall be over, and complete the sacred rite.

And now the day was waning, the mournfullest day this world has seen.

Joseph and Nicodemus have rolled the great round flagstone in its groove across the entrance of the dark and silent chamber. The Maries—she of Magdala, and the wife of Cleopas—have prepared their spices and their ointments. Nay, but had not one forestalled them? Their namesake, who six days before had anointed His body beforehand for His burial,—where was she? In her chamber, in her home at Bethany, near the empty seat which He had filled—He, the Resurrection and the Life—how those words must have filled her thoughts, and Lazarus by her side! And that one other, the Virgin Mother, blessed beyond them all, sorrowing beyond them all, widowed, childless, where is she? With Salome, in the house of the beloved Apostle. And the rest, where are they? With fainting hearts where they have severally concealed themselves. And so the Sabbath passes, all 'resting according to the commandment,' 'mourning and weeping,' St. Mark tells us, for it seemed to most of them as though all hope was at an end. They hoped up to the very last that it was He who should have redeemed Israel. But all was over; crushed, defeated, by the malice of bad men. In their deep revulsion of feeling all recollection of His words about rising again—never rightly understood—had passed away from their minds. The Pharisees who had heard the report of His having spoken such words, and feared some deception, need not have been so careful to seal and guard the tomb! And so the Sabbath passed.

Early on the first day of the week, before the sun had risen, the sky just reddening perhaps above the ridge of Olivet, the two Maries set forth, with the ointments they had prepared, towards the garden outside the city walls, questioning, as they walked along the silent streets, whom they should get to remove for them the heavy stone with which the cave was closed. And, behold, when they arrive the stone is gone, and the vault is open! The four soldiers who had been set to guard it in answer to their anxious questions tell them how there had been a quaking of the ground, and how, like a flash of light, an angel had descended and rolled away the stone.

But Mary Magdalene, either mistrusting or not waiting for their account, was already on her way back into the city to seek St. Peter and St. John, and tell them her fears that rude hands had violated her Lord's grave. The other women—Joanna and Salome had now joined them—now drew nearer, and perceived in the opening of the rocky chamber, seated on the stone, an angel in bright clothing, the same who had so dazzled and frightened the soldiers. 'Fear not ye,' he said, 'ye are seeking Jesus the crucified; He is not here; for He is risen, as He said. Come hither and see the place where the Lord lay.' And as the women stoop and look within they become aware that there is another angel also. But they must not tarry. 'Go quickly,' the angel says, 'and tell His disciples that He is risen from the dead: and, behold, He goeth before you into Galilee. There shall ye behold Him. Lo! I have told you!'

Hastily the women now returned to Jerusalem in mingled joy and fear.
Meantime by another road came St. Peter and St. John in haste, Mary Magdalene returning with them, but unable to keep pace. And John did outrun Peter; and stooping down under the low entrance to the vault, saw the linen clothes lying, but went not in. Then came up his bolder companion and went in, and found the linen clothes lying, and the napkin which had been about the head not lying with the clothes, but wrapped together in a place by itself. So careful had been the ministry of those attendant angels when the Lord of Glory rose. Then went in St. John also, and was convinced. For, as he himself confesses, up to that moment they had never understood the Scriptures which predicted the Resurrection.

The two Apostles now returned to their home in the city. But Mary Magdalene, who had by this time arrived, remained behind at the door of the tomb weeping, and drawing near, she too now stooped down to look into the chamber. And she beheld—what the lower spiritual sensibility of the two men had failed to see— the two angels, the same two angels, in their white apparel, sitting, one at the head and one at the foot, where the body of their Lord had lain. And they say unto her, 'Woman, why weepest thou?' She saith unto them, 'Because they have taken away my Lord, and I know not where they have laid Him.' And just then she heard a voice behind her repeating the same question, and, half looking round, supposed it was the gardener,—blinded by her tears and by the bright vision of the angels,—and said unto Him, 'Sir, if thou have borne Him hence, tell me where thou hast laid Him, and I will take Him away.' Jesus saith unto her, 'Mary.' She turned herself quite round and saith, 'Rabboni,' that is, my Master ! and would have clasped His knees ; for now that she has regained her Lord she feels as if she could never leave Him. But Jesus saith unto her, 'Touch me not, for I have not yet ascended unto My Father,'—these bodily appearances were not that return to abide with them for ever which He had promised them,—'but go and tell My brethren that I am ascending to My Father and your Father, and My God and your God !' As though His one thought now were a longing desire to ascend to His Father ; till then His joy is incomplete.

Meantime, the other women were on their way into the city. To them too Christ now appeared; or possibly St. Matthew, in recording the appearance to the women, is only noticing more generally that appearance to *one* of their number, which St. John has described in such minute detail. The way in which Cleopas and his companion speak afterwards of the tidings brought by the women (Luke xxiv. 23) seems to render this latter explanation the more probable.

The guards now went to the chief priests and told them all ; and the priests refer the matter to the Sanhedrim, who agree to bribe the soldiers to say that the disciples came by night and stole the body while they slept.

The women, rejoined by Mary Magdalene, now tell the rest of the Apostles—the nine who had not been to the garden—all that they have seen ; but their words seem to them as idle tales, and they believed them not.

CHAPTER XIV

The Forty Days

ONE appearance of the risen Christ we have recounted,—the appearance to Mary Magdalene.

His second appearance, how or where we know not, was to St. Peter. Not directly, but indirectly only, is it told us. We find St. Paul distinctly mentioning it in the 15th of 1st Corinthians : ' He was seen of Cephas, then of the Twelve.' Our first thought may be,—How strange that it should not be recorded by the four Evangelists! Is it not recorded? When those two returned from Emmaus to the upper chamber, where the rest were gathered together, what was the greeting with which they were received,—'The Lord is risen indeed, and hath appeared to *Simon*,'—one of those many undesigned coincidences which help to rivet our conviction of Holy Scripture's authenticity.

The third appearance was in the afternoon of this same Easter-day. Two disciples, Cleopas and another, neither of them Apostles, were walking to a village called Emmaus, seven or eight miles from Jerusalem ; and they talked together as they went of all that had been happening ; and as they talked and reasoned, Jesus Himself drew near and joined them in their walk. But their eyes were holden that they should not recognise Him. And He said unto them, ' What manner of communications are these that ye have one to another as ye walk and are sad?' And Cleopas answered, 'Art Thou the only visitor at Jerusalem who knows not what things have happened there in these last few days?' And He said, 'What things?' And they said, 'About Jesus, the mighty prophet of Nazareth, and how our priests and rulers delivered Him over to the Romans for crucifixion. Howbeit we, His disciples, were hoping that He was the promised Redeemer of Israel. Yea, and beside all this, to-day is the third day since His death' (a day that He more than once pointed to, as to be marked by some wonder): 'and what is more, some women of our company surprised us, who went early this morning to the sepulchre and found His body gone, and came back saying they had seen a vision of angels who said that He was alive. And certain of them that were with us went to the sepulchre, and found it even as the women said: but Him they saw not.'

Then the Stranger said to them :—' O foolish and slow of heart to believe all that the prophets spake ! Were not these the sufferings through which your Messiah was destined to pass into His glory ?'

Then He went through the types and prophecies of the Old Testament, showing how all, not merely the prophecies, but also the whole sacrificial system of Moses, pointed to this deep truth, that the Messiah must thus *suffer*, and yet *live* for ever.

They were by this time near to Emmaus, and their Companion was taking leave of them as though going further, but they pressed Him to abide with them, for it was now late in the afternoon ; and He consented. And now the three are at their evening meal, the mysterious Stranger and the two disciples, their eyes still holden ; when, lo, the look, the attitude they knew so well,—taking the bread, and blessing it, and breaking it, and giving it to each. Yes ! it is even He, —' their eyes were opened, and they knew Him.' And He vanished from their sight !

No wonder they had felt from the first that there was a mystery about this Stranger's presence ! ' Did not our hearts burn within us while He talked with us by the way, and while He opened to us the Scripture ? ' So one to the other, with bated breath, still gazing at the vacant place. But they must return, that very hour they must return to the Apostles at Jerusalem, with this great news. Two hours would bring them to Jerusalem. By eight o'clock they are in the upper chamber,—they find it filled, they find it hushed, the holy women, all are there ; their news has been forestalled : the Lord had appeared, while they were absent, had appeared to one of the Apostles, to Simon Peter. We must mark this, mark everything which throws light on the mysterious nature of these appearances : the Lord had appeared during their absence, possibly, probably at that very moment when he vanished at Emmaus. Oh! the deep emotion of those mutual greetings, ' The Lord is risen !' Yes, ' the Lord is risen indeed !' And as they compare notes and recount all, in their upper chamber, within their closed doors, now late in the evening, suddenly they become aware that He of whom they speak, the Lord Jesus, is Himself among them, saying, ' Peace be unto you !'

' Terrified and affrighted'—these sudden appearances, so unlike the intercourse of other days—they suppose it is some ghostly apparition. And yet the voice is the same voice, ' Why are ye troubled ? and why do questionings arise in your hearts ? Behold my hands and my feet, that it is I myself. Handle Me and see; for a spirit hath not flesh and bones as ye see Me have!' Then He showed them His hands and His feet—those pierced hands and feet; so mercifully patient, so gently reassuring. Ay and more, while they yet believe not for joy, and wonder, yet more will He do for their conviction: the remainder of their evening meal, the broiled fish and honeycomb, being still on their table, He took it and did eat before them all.

Then turning to them all, to the ten Apostles, to the two from Emmaus, to the holy women, to the rest, He blessed that infant Church, with a blessing far more solemn than any heretofore, even with a foretaste of that Holy Comforter Whom He had promised, perhaps in that selfsame upper chamber, three days before, breathing upon them with the warm human breath of His incarnation, and saying, 'Receive ye the Holy Ghost'—that Holy Spirit by whose aid the assembled Church was to have the power of binding and of loosing, of admitting and refusing membership in her divine communion.

Thus four times at least on this day of Resurrection did our Lord manifest Himself bodily to His disciples, —to the Magdalene, to Simon Peter, to the two at Emmaus, to the rest in the upper chamber.

One week longer the Apostles tarried at Jerusalem, the feast of the Passover being not yet over, and on the Sunday following we hear of them as being again assembled in their upper chamber, with closed doors for fear of the Sanhedrim; and this time Thomas is with them: on that first day he had been absent. Again Christ appears to them supernaturally, saying, ' Peace be unto you!' and vouchsafes to the doubting one, to Thomas, the same evidence of hand and side whereby the others had been convinced. 'Reach hither thy finger, and behold my hands; and reach hither thy hand, and thrust it into my side: and be not faithless, but believing.' 'Wounded for our transgression,'—those wounds still open, albeit healed,—Thomas looks 'on Him whom they had pierced,' and weak in faith, yet faithful in his weakness, pours forth his adoration, 'My Lord and my God.'

Nor does the everlasting Son of God refuse his worship; but accepts it rather as the prelude of an ever-widening hymn of praise,—' Thomas, because thou hast seen thou hast believed: blessed are they that have not seen and yet have believed.' Even as He had prayed before His passion: 'Neither pray I for these alone, but for them also who shall believe on Me through their word.'

Such was our Lord's fifth appearance.

How long after this we know not certainly, but probably *at once* (the Passover being now completely over), the Apostles, by our Lord's direction, returned to the neighbourhood of Capernaum, where most of them had homes. Seven of them, at Simon Peter's suggestion, betook themselves to their old means of support as fishermen. In this we are reminded that He, to Whom the holy women had ministered so abundantly of their substance, was now no longer sharing the necessities of their daily life. Without Him they could not claim that ministration. In the twilight of the early dawn, after a night of fruitless toil, they see some one standing on the beach, a hundred yards off, calling to them. He asks them, as a passing stranger might, what success they had had in their fishing, and bids them cast the net on the right side of the boat; and forthwith they enclose a great multitude of fishes. Ah, how vividly is that day brought to the mind of one of them, that day when he was first called to be a fisher of men ! St. John was the first to recognise the Lord, and to his friend he exclaims, ' It is the Lord !' St. Peter, ever foremost, swims to shore, the rest follow with the net. On the beach they find a charcoal fire with bread and meat—whence they knew not ; in the greater mystery of His presence the lesser mystery was lost. Nor durst they question, ' knowing it was the Lord.'

Solemnly as before He breaks the bread, and gives it them. Then, turning to St. Peter, yet humbled by his fall, He commissions him anew to feed His sheep, and foretells his martyrdom before the great downfall of the nation,—that first coming of the Son of Man to judgment, which St. John should live to see.

This was Christ's sixth appearance. A seventh was on the mountain of Galilee, where St. Matthew tells us He had appointed them to meet Him : the greatest, in one sense, of all the appearances, for here probably were gathered together those five hundred disciples whom St. Paul mentions as permitted also to be eye-witnesses of the Resurrection. And here, too, Christ proclaimed His universal kingdom : 'All power is given unto Me in heaven and in earth : Go ye, therefore, and Christianize all nations, baptizing them into the Name of the Father, the Son, and the Holy Ghost.'—Reader ! dost thou recognise the full significance of this Divine formula, now for the first time heard on earth ? To realize the awe with which those Apostles must have heard it, bethink thee of the absolute impossibility of conceiving any other name this world has ever named being placed in the second place of that mystic Trinity ! Then thou wilt realize the claim now heard by the

The Forty Days

Apostles from the lips of Him with Whom they had so often broken bread !

One more, the last, of these appearances remains : for that to St. James, the Lord's brother, may be passed over ; the bare fact and nothing more is recorded by St. Paul. But to the eleven Apostles one further sign is to be vouchsafed. To three only had the first Transfiguration been granted. All the Apostles are to behold this second and yet greater Transfiguration. The approaching feast of Pentecost, it may be, or our Lord's command, had drawn them once more to the Holy City. There the Lord meets them, ten days before the feast, and conducts them, as of old, across the Kedron, and up the sloping sides of Olivet, even towards that well-loved home at Bethany. As they go Christ sums up all His teaching, pointing onwards to the ever-widening spread of His gospel, silencing their curiosity about the times and seasons, repeating His promise of the blessed Comforter, bidding them abide in Jerusalem until that Comforter should come. And then, as He raised His hands in act to bless them, He was parted from them, and slowly rose from earth towards heaven, disappearing into the well-known cloud of glory, the symbol of Jehovah's presence. And as they gazed and gazed, behold, two men stood by them in white apparel, which also said, ' Ye men of Galilee, why stand ye gazing up into heaven ? This same Jesus which is taken up from you into heaven, shall so come in like manner as ye have seen Him go into heaven !'

Till then He is behind the veil !

PART III
Notes on the Gospel Narrative

CHAPTER I
On the Narrative of the Birth and Infancy

WHAT is the chief lesson of this curiously detailed narrative of the Birth and Infancy of Christ?

Suppose we had it not; suppose Christmas with all its lovely memories was cut out from our Christian year; suppose all four Gospels had commenced as St. Mark's commences, with Christ's baptism in Jordan at thirty years of age, and all before was blank :—no angel's salutation, no mystery of birth, no pastoral symphony, no star-led wizards, no inspired canticles, no glimpse of that daily growth in wisdom as in stature; but all blank, until the Baptist cried aloud and said, 'There is One among you whom ye know not!'—what then would have been our creed? what would have been the creed, I do not say of the sceptic or rationalist, but of the devout Christian, of the Christian Church?

Clearly, and, as it seems to me, inevitably this: that the time for the Messiah's advent being fully come, God looked down from heaven upon the children of men, and singled out one, an Israelite indeed, in whom there was no guile, and said, ' This shall be My Son, in whom I will be pleased that the fulness of My Spirit shall dwell:'—and that this child of man, thus perfected, thus developed by inspiration and by the anointing in Jordan into a Son of God, was enabled by Divine power to realize this ideal during some two or three years, was then crucified, raised again to life, and so disappeared.

Such almost inevitably would have been our creed, and such verses as John xvii. 5, which speaks of the glory which He had with the Father before the world was, or Col. i. 16 and Heb. i. 2, where He is spoken of as the Creator of the world, would be simply an inexplicable enigma.

In saying this I am not merely drawing on my own imagination. As early as the second century this heresy took root in the Christian Church. Accustomed from childhood to the fables of heathen mythology, men began to ask themselves whether it might not be that God, or some emanation from God, had entered into the man Jesus at his baptism, and so enabled him to do all those marvellous works. The notion gained ground rapidly, and took shape in the Gospel of Marcion. Marcion was an ardent admirer of Christ's teaching, a man of the most exemplary, even ascetic life. But in the creed of the Church he found difficulties, and to explain them away he framed his Gospel.

And what is this Gospel of Marcion? A mere mutilation of St. Luke's. And what portion specially of St. Luke did Marcion find it necessary to strike out? *These first two chapters*[1].

[1] Marcion's Gospel begins with the statement that in the

Yes, he who would attempt to rationalize the Gospel of Christ,—he who would persuade us that Jesus Christ was after all only *an ideal man*, into whom the divine element of Humanity entered so largely, and was so perfectly developed, that he became, as it were, the personification of all that is purest and noblest in our race,—he who would thus explain away the divinity of our Redeemer (our Redeemer no longer) by any such theory of human development, must begin at the beginning, must on the very threshold of the Gospel cut away and get rid of that simple holy tale of Bethlehem.

The manhood of Christ, and His miracles, all *that* his philosophy is able (as he thinks) to grapple with— for who shall limit the spiritual power of a perfected humanity?—all that he can deal with and idealize. But this mysterious birth, these clear attestations that the eternal Son of God was incarnate in that infant child of Mary, these exact fulfilments of ancient prophecy, these angel witnesses, this dawning consciousness of His divine origin,—if all this be really historical, then the sceptic's theory is destroyed, and his philosophy refuted. He who feared not to assail the Lord Christ is confounded before the holy child Jesus. Out of the mouth of the babe and suckling is ordained the strength that shall still the enemy and the avenger!

If any modern philosophy,—compelled to accept the rise of *Christianity* as a fact in the world's history 1800 years ago, but wishing to get rid of its supernatural origin,—ever whisper into our ears that the Christ whom we worship is *the ideal man*, whom the

fifteenth year of Tiberius, the Christ of God (*spiritus salutaris*) deigned to enter into Jesus in Capernaum.—Tertull. *adv. Marc.* i. 19 and iv. 7.

pious credulity of the Church loved to picture forth as having once walked this earth, clothing some guileless Jewish Rabbi with all conceivable excellences,— then, as we value our own spiritual comfort, let us cling to these simple Gospel facts which we learned at our mother's knee, and which all the historic criticism of our age is tending more and more to establish. Let us cling to our blessed Christmas memories of Nazareth and of Bethlehem, dear to our childhood, dearer to our maturer reason, teaching us more clearly, more persuasively, more convincingly than any systems of theology can teach, that He in Whom all our hopes are centred is in very truth a divine eternal personal Being, altogether distinct in His personality, above us and beyond us, and yet—that we might know Him and love Him—entering into the sphere of our finite history, incarnate by the Holy Ghost, born of a woman, sharing our very nature, bone of our bone, flesh of our flesh, breathing our breath, thinking our thoughts, feeling our infirmities, One Whom in childhood, One Whom in manhood we may know and love, living His divine life now beyond the grave, gone to prepare a place for us, warming with the warmth of a human heart, enlightening with the light of loving human eyes, that unseen world into which we are all hastening !

CHAPTER II

On the Silence of the Gospels respecting our Lord's Life at Nazareth

SURELY it is no small proof that one and the same Holy Spirit inspired and overruled these four Evangelists, that, writing as they did for very different readers,—one for the Jewish Church, another for that of Rome, a third for the Churches of Greece, a fourth for those of Asia Minor,—they should thus *all, with one accord*, pass over in complete silence more than nine-tenths of our Lord's earthly life.

Doubtless the faithful memory of *her* who kept and pondered all things in her heart, could have supplied to St. Luke, not only that one precious anecdote of the boyhood, but also numberless other anecdotes of the youth and early manhood of the deepest interest. How we long for them! What would we not give to know more of that home at Nazareth, where thirty long years of that sinless life were spent! But no! it is buried in silence. And why? The silence of Holy Scripture is often as instructive as its revelations,—let us humbly, therefore, learn the lesson of this mysterious silence.

There were inmates of that Galilean home to whom was vouchsafed, what is denied to us, the privilege of watching the growth of Jesus all through those silent years. And to them it once occurred, as now to us, to wonder that Jesus did not seek to make Himself more widely known. 'Show Thyself to the world,' they said. And what was Christ's reply? 'My time is not yet come: your time is always ready.'

And what is the Evangelist's own comment? 'For neither did His brethren believe on Him.'

Here, then, we have a lesson and a warning.

The lesson :—That God's ways are not as man's ways[1]—that whatever is most divine is most secret in its growth; as with the seed that groweth secretly, we know not how, as with the hidden life of grace within each one of us, so with the Messiah in His silent home at Nazareth ;—'it is the glory of God to conceal a thing'[2]. Such is the lesson.

And the warning :—That the kind of knowledge we most crave after is not always the kind of knowledge that is best for us. To those 'brethren of the Lord'—was their knowledge of Christ's daily life all through those years a blessing to them? No: 'for neither did His brethren believe on Him.' Let Bible students, in their curious antiquarian researches, ever remember this. To know all about Christ is one thing : to *know Christ* is quite another thing. Nay, the first kind of knowledge may, as in the case of those brethren, actually hinder the second. Let us beware, lest, by dwelling too minutely and exclusively on the earthly surroundings of our Lord, we dim to ourselves the glory of His divine Person. It was not flesh and blood which revealed to Peter that in Jesus of Nazareth he beheld the Son of the living God.

---

[1] So Tertullian, with us men '*subito* omnia, quæ suum et plenum habent ordinem apud Creatorem.'—*Adv. Marc.* iv. 11.   [2] Prov. xxv. 2.

This, then, is the warning :—That the Gospel narrative is not a biography, but rather a *revelation*. God grant it be so! God grant that to all of us the pages of these Gospels be no mere history, but ever more and more an open vision of the Son of God!

CHAPTER III

On the Narrative of the Temptation

WHERE so much that a mere biographer would have been sure to relate is withheld from us, surely it was for some deep purpose that this mysterious glimpse into the spiritual experiences of our blessed Lord, which no mere biographer could possibly have given us, was by God's inspiration revealed to us.

Three remarks may be made upon it.

We remark, first, that it was in all its circumstances *supernatural*.

Secondly, that we have here unanswerably revealed to us the *personal* existence of the Evil One; and

Thirdly, that in our Lord's manner of meeting these temptations, we may find a key to all that follows,— we may discern the *plan* or *scheme* which Christ had laid down for Himself, for the accomplishment of His work on earth.

On each of these three heads a few words of explanation are needed.

And first, the circumstances of this Temptation were *supernatural*.

Idle questions have been asked, whether our Lord really stood on a pinnacle of the Temple, and if so, how He had been taken thither out of the wilderness; and whether He really ascended a mountain, and if so, what mountain it was.

Idler questions could hardly be.

Let us remind ourselves what in after years befell two of the Apostles. St. John tells us that he was in the isle of Patmos on the Lord's day, and was 'in the Spirit.' What does this mean? Does it mean that he was lifted bodily up? No: the natural man was in the isle of Patmos the whole time; and yet he speaks of beholding Rome on its seven hills one while, and another while the river Euphrates, clearly in his state of spiritual trance. Again, St. Paul tells the Corinthians how he had been once 'caught up to the third heaven,' and once 'into Paradise.' Does he mean bodily? He forbids such idle questions: 'Whether in the body or out of the body, I cannot tell: God knoweth:' it was not a natural but a supernatural experience.

Clear it is that the soul of man is capable of other and higher experiences than those which his bodily faculties convey to him. Clear it is that it has pleased God, and may again please God, so to quicken our spiritual perceptions as to make us aware of that angelic world which is ever around us. Most clear it is that our blessed Lord was, all through His ministry, more or less in this state of 'open vision.' No one who is unwilling to believe this can understand the Gospel narrative.

Secondly, it is here distinctly revealed that the Evil One has a most real *personal* existence. In the Old Testament this is rarely declared; but in the New Testament it is so plainly asserted that none can deny it without attributing error to Christ and His Apostles.

Does it occur to those who venture to explain our Lord's constant allusions to the Evil One as a condescension to Hebrew modes of thought,—personifying the evil tendencies of our nature, just as *wisdom* is personified in the Book of Proverbs,—does it occur to them to consider the consequences of their theory when applied to this Temptation of our Lord in His solitude,—that all these sinful temptations came from within, not from without, from within His own all-holy nature? Such a notion only requires to be stated to be instantly rejected. If the devil have not an objective personal existence, Christ's Temptation is an impossibility, and the narrative of it an impious fabrication. But grant his personality, and not only is this narrative explained, but also a part of the mystery of Redemption begins dimly to reveal itself. For if it were *evil in the abstract* that Christ vanquished, 'twere hard to see how His victory could benefit unborn generations, except by way of example. But if it were *an Evil One*, then the power of that Evil One for all after time was maimed and broken, waiting only one more final conflict to be crushed and destroyed for ever.

This we rejoice to believe: but let us remember our belief in this aspect of Redemption is bound up with our belief in Satan's personality.

Thirdly and lastly, we come to Christ's *divine plan* or *scheme* as shadowed forth in this conflict.

Three things herein may be observed:—His attitude of filial obedience, not 'what I will,' but 'what My Father wills' throughout. Again, His self-sacrifice,—not a single miracle in His own behalf. And again, His refusal of an outward kingdom.

How clearly the broad lines of His divine purpose are here laid down! and how it helps to explain all that follows!

To revive in the world, what the world had well-nigh lost, the consciousness of God : to sacrifice His outward life, that He might so pass, in this self-revealing consciousness, into the inward life of men : to build up on this basis, and none other, that kingdom of God which is at once outside us and within us :— such, and no less, was the divine plan of Christ.

In connexion with what I have ventured to call 'the divine plan' of Christ, there is another point which must be carefully borne in mind by one who would rightly understand the Gospel narrative. It is this :—

Christ came to be the *subject*, rather than the *author*, of Christianity.

Christianity, as a religion and as a church, dates, not from Christmas, nor yet from the Ministry, but from Pentecost. It was the work of the Third, rather than of the Second Person of the ever-blessed Trinity. Our Lord came to redeem the world, and to atone for sin. He had a baptism of suffering to be baptized with ; and till that was accomplished, His teaching and His ministry were straitened (Luke xii. 50).

This *straitening* of Christ in His ministry—as one speaking to men still under the *old*, not yet under the *new*, dispensation, with much need therefore of reserve—must be borne in mind by all readers of our Lord's discourses. It explains too the often repeated charge not to make Him known.

When once He was exalted to God's right hand, all need of this reserve ceased. It is to the later books of the New Testament, therefore, rather than to the Gospels, that we must look for the development of the doctrine and organization of the Church.

CHAPTER IV

On Our Lord's Miracles

THE common objection to the credibility of miracles, as old as Hume and older, is this :—A miracle is a violation of the laws of nature ; and as all human experience has established the constancy of those laws, it must always be more likely that testimony should be mistaken than that a miracle should have occurred.

The answer is a very simple one :—A miracle is *not* 'a violation of the laws of nature ;' it is simply the revelation of a superhuman agent, possessing superhuman powers, and therefore *not included under the rules generalized from human experience*[1].

To one who believes in the existence of such a superhuman Agent, and in the probability of His willing to make a special revelation of Himself to mankind, this answer must be entirely satisfactory.

Without going further, therefore, into this question, let us humbly and reverently endeavour to draw out the chief lessons which our Lord's miracles were designed to teach.

[1] It is much to be regretted that the writer of the article on Miracles in *Aids to Faith* should inadvertently have used the phrase, 'introduction of a *new* agent, possessing *new* powers.' The novelty was not the presence of a Divine Power in the world, but the revelation of it.

Our Lord's miracles were revelations. A revelation is the lifting of a veil. Our Lord, in these miracles, lifted a veil, as it were; and allowed mankind to see, what had ever been going on behind it, the working of Divine Power. It was but for a few short years. The veil was then again lowered. And the Church was thenceforth required to believe by faith, what had been thus revealed, the continued working of the Divine Power behind the veil.

That Christ should be able thus to lift the veil, or (to drop the metaphor) to give men these new experiences, was a clear proof of His divinity. For no mere man could do it. 'If I had not done among them the works which none other man did, they had not had sin: but now have they both seen and hated both Me and My Father.'

To identify Himself with His Father, by showing that He could do visibly what His Father was ever doing invisibly, was doubtless the first great purpose of Christ's miracles. So far from wishing men to regard His miracles as contrary to the laws of nature, Christ was careful to teach the very opposite lesson —the perfect harmony of His mode of working, in these miracles, with God's mode of working in what is called the ordinary course of nature:—'My Father worketh hitherto, and I work;' 'The Son can do nothing of Himself but what He seeth the Father do; for what things soever the Father doeth, these things doeth the Son likewise.'

Instead, therefore, of presuming to say, 'I understand God's ordinary mode of working in nature, and these miracles of Christ are quite unlike it, and therefore incredible:'—let us rather confess that there is much of mystery in nature, and see what light these miracles of Christ may throw upon it. And that they do throw a most blessed light on what, after all, we most wish to know about this world in which we live, will more and more appear, the more attentively we study them.

Our Lord's miracles, with this view, may be conveniently divided into three groups :—

I. The great draughts of fishes, the calming of the storm, the withering of the fig-tree. These miracles, it will be observed, involve nothing new, but only a providential arrangement of natural events. For shortness' sake, they may be called '*providential.*'

II. The walking on the sea, the change of water into wine, the multiplication of the loaves, the cure of infirmities humanly speaking incurable. Here a new and strange experience was introduced; all these miracles belonged to the world of nature, and yet were *beside* nature,—men had never seen the like before. They may be called, for shortness, '*preternatural.*'

III. The expulsion of demons, and the recall of the departed human spirit. These miracles, as belonging to a world above and beyond the world of nature, may most properly be termed '*supernatural.*'

Now let us endeavour to learn the three lessons taught severally by these three classes of miracles.

I. Of the miracles of the first class it has been already remarked that they involved in their results nothing new or foreign to our ordinary experience. Often and often before had men's efforts to obtain their livelihood been unusually prospered, storms calmed, fruits of the earth blighted. Such occurrences were common. But men had observed, or thought they had observed, indications of design, of moral purpose, in these occurrences. Was it so, or was it not? If it was so, then the world was governed not by chance or fate, but by a personal Providence ; and if so, *prayer* was a possibility.

Clearly a momentous question ; and one to which it was highly probable that Christ would give an answer. And how better could Christ answer it, than by giving a specimen of such special providence, in which, not only the result, but also He who willed that result, should be *visible ?* And this was precisely what Christ did in this first group of miracles: —' Lord save us, we perish !' Often and often before had the prayer been uttered to One unseen, in the *hope* that such an unseen One was ruling the event. But here the whole process was laid bare, and the special providence stood revealed :—' And He arose, and rebuked the wind, and the wind ceased, and there was a great calm.'

Let none say that such special providences are incompatible with the constancy of nature's laws. This world of ours is like an organ,—not a barrel-organ (to which the fatalist would liken it), but a key-board organ,—on which, without violating one of those laws under which the forces of the organ act, the organist may play what melody he will ; the wish of a child may change the tune. Even so this system of forces, to which we give the name of nature, is sufficiently elastic (as we know by daily experience) to allow room for our free will,—and if for man's free will, then much more for God's free will,—and if so, then for special providence and prayer.

Such, we may reverently believe, was the special lesson about nature revealed in this first group of our Lord's miracles.

II. But granting the existence of such a Divine Will arranging and disposing nature's forces, a further question about nature, of infinite concern to us, remains :—Which is *sovereign*, God or nature?

The human will, although it has a kind of sovereignty (the very expression 'free will' implying as much), acts, nevertheless, under limitations, and these limitations are imposed by nature. ' Natura non nisi parendo vincitur :'—Nature to be commanded must be obeyed[1] :—Bacon's Aphorism well expresses the limitation imposed by the constant laws of nature on the human will. Man's will is free to *dispose* her forces (though this only mediately—through the intervention of his own bodily organization), but it can neither increase nor diminish nature's constant amount of energy[2],—can neither create nor destroy.

Is it so with God's Will? If it be so, then nature is co-ordinate and co-eternal with God.

Recoiling instinctively from such nature-worship, men always trusted they might still believe in the absolute supremacy of a Personal Will,—believe that behind the Law there was a Lawgiver.

But how could this be proved? How could our Lord best bring it home to the conviction of the Galilean peasant, and of the simple folk of His Church in all ages?

How better than by destroying (for the moment) some force of nature, creating some new matter, restoring some lost energy, before men's eyes?

In walking on the water, in supplying bread and

[1] *Nov. Org.* i. 1.
[2] For a discussion of the modern doctrine of the *conservation of force* in its relation to *free will*, see Sir John Herschel's essay 'on the origin of force,' in his *Lectures on Scientific Subjects*.

wine, in renewing sight and health, Christ gave men glimpses of creative power.

To think of these acts as violations of nature's laws, is a confusion of thought; to create or destroy a force is not to violate the law under which that force acts.

As, therefore, in the first group of miracles Christ revealed God as the Sovereign Disposer of nature's forces, so in this second group He revealed God as the Sovereign Creator and possible Destroyer of those forces.

III. But granting this absolute sovereignty of God over nature, there was yet another question on which we needed a revelation.

Man is conscious of living in another world besides the world of nature. Joy and sorrow, right and wrong, love and hate, have never yet been weighed in the naturalist's balance or analysed by his prism. They are the forces of another world entirely distinct from that of nature, supernatural, the world of personality and spirit. In that other world we are conscious of living; and what is more, in that other world, something whispers, we shall continue to live, still subject to its forces, when to the world of nature we have died. Is God's will sovereign there also?

This, too, Christ would reveal. To this other supernatural world the miracles of the third class belong.

In the case of expelling demons this is self-evident. In raising the dead, a moment's consideration will show that the miracle was wrought not on the body[1], but on the spirit of the departed.

---

[1] If, along with the recall of the spirit, there was also a change wrought in the body, a healing of its mortification, this was a distinct miracle belonging to our second group,

In all the three recorded instances there was, it may be observed, a kind of refusal on our Lord's part to regard the *person* as dead :—'The damsel is not dead but sleepeth ;' 'Whosoever liveth and believeth in Me shall never die.' So the summons was ever as to one who could yet hear His voice :—'Damsel, I say unto thee, arise ;' 'Young man, I say unto thee, arise ;' 'Lazarus, come forth.' In all three instances it seemed to be our Lord's wish to reveal Himself as the 'Lord both of the dead and living ;' for, in His own words, 'all live unto Him.'

These miracles of the third class, therefore, were spiritual not physical ; they belonged to a region into which the laws of nature do not enter, and therefore in no way contravened them ; and in that higher region they revealed the sovereignty of God.

To sum up what has been said. All Christ's miracles—whether providential, or preternatural, or supernatural—were visible manifestations of a Divine Power which is ever working in the two worlds in which we live and have our being.

They were, at once, both self-revelations, and also revelations about God.

They were self-revelations ; for that Christ should be able, in His own Person, to vouchsafe such manifestations of Divine Power, proved Himself Divine.

They were also revelations about God, for they were specimens of God's mode of working.

That God works, in nature, through certain forces, and that the action of these forces is uniform,—this no miracle was needed to reveal ; God is revealing it and would by no means have sufficed alone for the restoration of life.

to us all by daily experience,—never so wonderfully as in these later days to the students of His works. Without such uniformity providence on man's part would be impossible.[1]

But that these uniformities are compatible with special Providence and prayer; that 'Causation is the Will, Creation the act, of God';[2] that the world of spirit and the world of nature are governed by one and the same Heavenly Father;—these were truths of which no philosophy, no science, could assure us. They are revealed to us in the miracles of our Lord.

[1] Such is the explanation which suggested itself to Butler's strong practical sense (*Analogy*, i. 7). No less characteristic is that of Pascal, that God veils the freedom of His will under these uniformities, to leave room for faith :—' Si Dieu se découvrait continuellement aux hommes, il n'y aurait point de mérite à le croire ; et s'il ne se découvrait jamais, il y aurait peu de foi.'—*Pensées* II., xvi. 8.

[2] With these noble words, Mr. Grove concludes his essay on the *Correlation of Physical Forces*,—reminding us of Bacon, where he tells us that, 'so far is the study of physical causes from withdrawing men from God and Providence, that, on the contrary, those who have occupied themselves in searching them out, have never been able to find the end of the matter, without having recourse at length to the doctrine of Divine Providence.'—*De Aug.* iii. 4.

CHAPTER V

Christ's Death a Mystery.

NO one can read the Gospel narrative without seeing that there was a deep significance in Christ's sufferings and death. The purpose of this chapter is to show how clearly this is implied in the four Gospels,—taken alone, and without recourse to the more doctrinal statements of the Epistles.

1. And, first, Christ's death was a *martyrdom:* Christ died a martyr to the truth of His Divinity.

This comes out very plainly in the account of the two trials. Christ was arraigned in the Jewish Court on the charge of Blasphemy, and condemned. Christ was then arraigned in the Roman Court on the charge of Treason, and acquitted. Failing in this second accusation, the Jews fell back on the first, and persuaded Pilate to execute the sentence of their own Court. Thus Christ was executed because He had ' spoken blasphemy.'

But what was the blasphemy? and how was it proved?

The blasphemy was that ' He made Himself the Son of God;'—'We have a law, and by our law He ought to die, because He made Himself the Son of God.'

And how was it proved? Other evidence failing, the Prisoner was adjured, or put upon oath, by the

High Priest, 'I adjure Thee by the living God that Thou tell us whether Thou be the Christ, the Son of God.' Not the Messiah merely (possibly that would not have been accounted blasphemy), but also 'the Son of God;' St. Luke gives them as two separate questions. Christ accepted the oath, and declared that He was. And that this declaration was understood at the time in the full sense in which the Church has ever understood it, is abundantly proved by what followed[1].

If Christ had recalled or qualified His words, when He found them thus understood, He would not have been condemned; but He allowed them to stand, to stand for all ages, as a most solemn assertion of His Divinity.

He died, therefore, a martyr to this truth. Never was the mystery of His Person so clearly revealed as in the process of His death.

2. There was in Christ's Passion an *agony* which the mere painfulness of the death cannot possibly account for.

This, too, plainly appears from the narrative.

As the hour approached, the agony of His inward sufferings crushed Him to the earth, strained to the very uttermost His human power of endurance.

Contrast this with what we know of the last hours of many of His saints, of the Stephens, Polycarps, Ridleys, Latimers, of later days. Many of them endured torture of body far greater than that of crucifixion; and yet they met their death unflinchingly, even cheerfully,—without any such agony.

Clearly Christ's agony implies that there was far more than appeared, a deep mystery, in His sufferings.

[1] See pages 81 and 93.

3. Christ's sufferings were *fore-ordained.* This is again and again insisted on, not only by the Evangelists, but by our Lord Himself, when training His disciples' minds to understand the mystery of His death. Before the idea of putting Him to death had entered into the heart of a single Jew, we find it vividly present to the mind of Christ. Within two months of His Baptism He was speaking of it, yea, and of the very manner of it, to Nicodemus :—'As Moses lifted up the serpent in the wilderness, even so must the Son of Man be lifted up.' Not only did our Lord, on three several occasions, predict the very circumstances,—the betrayal, the condemnation by the priests, the delivery to the Romans, the scourging, the crucifixion, the Resurrection on the third day,— but He carefully traced this fore-ordained purpose all through the Old Testament Scriptures ; referring not to a few isolated texts, but to all that was 'written in the law of Moses, and in the prophets, and in the Psalms' concerning Him.

Now here we have a great help towards understanding the mystery of the Death. For how is it to be traced all through the law of Moses ? Plainly and necessarily in the sacrificial system of that law. Christ can have meant nothing else ; for of direct prediction of the Messiah's death there is not in the books of Moses a single word.

4. Christ's death was therefore a *sacrifice.* And if so, what a light this throws on the agony of the suffering,—if there was really laid upon Him, in some mysterious way, the sin of mankind ! For this was to a Jew's mind, to the Apostles' minds therefore, the essential notion of a sacrifice. A sacrifice was *a freewill-offering for the expiation of sin.*

I

Now both parts of this twofold idea are expressly connected with Christ's death in the Gospels.

Again and again Christ impressed it on His disciples' minds that His approaching death was a *free-will-offering*:—'I am the good shepherd : the good shepherd giveth his life for the sheep.' 'Therefore doth My Father love Me, because I lay down My life.' . . . 'No man taketh it from Me, but I lay it down of Myself. I have power to lay it down, and I have power to take it again.' 'Thinkest thou that I cannot now pray to My Father, and He shall presently give Me more than twelve legions of angels? But how then shall the Scriptures be fulfilled, that thus it must be?' 'Not My will, but Thine, be done !'

So, also, again and again, it is implied that Christ's death was an *expiation* for the sin of the world :— 'Behold the Lamb of God which taketh away the sin of the world.' 'The Son of Man must be lifted up, that whosoever believeth in Him should not perish, but have eternal life.' 'If any man eat of this bread he shall live for ever, and the bread that I will give is My flesh, which I will give for the life of the world.' 'The Son of Man came to give His life a ransom for many.' 'This is My body which is given for you.' . . . 'This is My blood of the new covenant, which is shed for many for the remission of sins.' 'For their sakes I sanctify (or consecrate) Myself.' The sacrificial allusion in all these passages is unmistakable.

5. But there is yet one more mystery connected with Christ's sufferings. There are clear indications in the Gospel narrative that those sufferings involved *a conflict*, a final conflict, *with the Evil One*. And if so, again what a light is thrown on that agony in Gethsemane !

And is it not so? After the Temptation, when the Devil left Him, it is added that it was 'for a season' only. And when did he return? In Gethsemane; for Christ declared it on His way thither :—'The Prince of this world cometh, and hath nothing in Me;' and again, 'this is your hour and the power of darkness.'

There is another ground for supposing that in the Garden the conflict of the Wilderness was renewed: —twice, and twice only, do we read of an angel ministering to Christ, after the Temptation, and after the Agony. May we not see here an indication that in both a victory had been won? And with this thought I would venture to connect those words recorded by St. John[1] only :—'Father, save Me from this hour.' . . . 'Father, glorify Thy name' (by giving Me the victory over the Evil One); then came there a voice from heaven, 'I have both glorified and will glorify it again' (once by the victory in the wilderness, once again by the victory in Gethsemane).

Thus, to sum up, it is evident from our Gospel record, that Christ's Passion was not only a *martyrdom*, but also a most mysterious *agony*, the fulfilment of a *fore-ordained* purpose, a *sacrifice*, and a *conflict* with the Evil One. That there was all this deep mystery in it, was plainly revealed, as we have seen, by Christ to His Apostles, even before the Pentecostal gift of the Holy Spirit enabled them to comprehend the full doctrine of the Atonement which in that Death was once for all accomplished.

[1] John xii. 27, 28.

CHAPTER VI

On the Chronology of the Gospel Narrative

IT has been well said[1] that the main purpose of the four Evangelists was not so much to write chronicles, as to set forth such an account of the sayings and doings of our Lord as might best prove Him to be the Messiah. This purpose governs, not only their *selection*, but also to some extent their *grouping*, of the incidents. This will be plain to any one who compares the order of the events of the Galilean ministry as told by St. Matthew, on the one hand, with the order of the same events as told by St. Mark and St. Luke, on the other[2]. Hence the difficulties of the harmonist. But, in the midst of these difficulties, one is ever comforted by the thought that the matter is one of altogether secondary importance.

One who studies these four divine portraitures with

[1] By Tischendorf in the Prolegomena of his *Synopsis Evangelica*. To this work, and to the treatise of Wieseler, on which it is based, I need hardly say how deeply I am indebted; and still more, perhaps, to Bishop Ellicott's *Historical Lectures*, which first led me to study the Gospel arrangement of Wieseler. Where I have ventured to depart from his order of events it has been with much diffidence, and only because I gave yet greater weight to the opinion of some of the early Fathers.

[2] See the Table on page 142, for the events of A.D. 28, Jan., Feb., and March, observing the regular sequence of chapters in the *Mark* and *Luke* columns, and the irregularity of the *Matthew* column, noted by the asterisks.

the view of compiling from them a dry chronicle, is studying them with a purpose far lower than that with which they were written ; nor must he be disappointed if he fail. *If we knew all*, we could certainly reconcile their apparent inconsistencies ; *not knowing all*, we may well expect to find it impossible.

The tabular view, therefore, which is appended to this chapter, is given, not for one moment as a complete harmony, but merely as a useful index, presenting to the reader's eye, in a form convenient for reference, the arrangement of the leading facts adopted in the narrative portion of this volume.

It needs but little explanation.

The dates given in the first column[1] result almost necessarily from the assumption made throughout this book that our Lord was born *four* complete years before the Dionysian or vulgar era ; that He had just completed His *thirtieth* year at His baptism ; and that His Ministry lasted two years and a quarter.

In justification of these assumptions, a few words may be desired by my more studious readers.

I. *The year of our Lord's birth.*—St. Matthew's Gospel makes it plain that the Nativity took place about three months[2] before Herod's death ; and the date of Herod's death is fortunately fixed for us by the eclipse of the moon which Josephus[3] mentions as occurring during his last illness. Astronomers give the 13th of March in the year of Rome 750, or B.C. 4,

[1] Where the *day* of the month is given, it is on the authority of the Tables of full moons, furnished by astronomers.

[2] Between the Nativity and Herod's death we must allow forty days for the Purification (Lev. xii.), and time (after that) for the flight into Egypt and sojourn there.

[3] *Ant.* xvii. 6. 4.

as the date of this eclipse. As Herod died before the Passover (12th April), the date of the Nativity is thus thrown back to the very beginning of B.C. 4, or to the end of B.C. 5[1].

II. *The date of the Baptism.*—This is carefully defined by St. Luke. It seems to me that his words can only bear one construction, that our Lord was just completing His thirtieth year[2]. The Baptism must, therefore, be dated early in A.U.C. 780, or A.D. 27.

III. *The duration of the Ministry.*—The solution of this question must be sought in St. John's Gospel.

Any one, carefully following the notes of time afforded by his first four chapters, will see that the Feast mentioned in the first verse of the fifth chapter must have occurred within fifteen months of the Baptism. On this point nearly all commentators are agreed.

Again, all are agreed that the Feast of Tabernacles, mentioned in his seventh chapter, must have been within seven months of the Crucifixion.

The duration of the ministry depends, therefore, on the length of the interval between these two feasts, or (in other words) between the fifth and seventh chapters of St. John.

The close and intimate connexion of these two chapters convinces me that this interval cannot have been a long one, certainly not more than six or seven months.

In the fifth chapter our Lord cures an impotent man

---

[1] For all this see Wieseler's *Chron. Synopse*, p. 56.

[2] 'The Greek Fathers, who must have understood their own language best, never took these words to mean anything else.'—Greswell, Dissert. xi. Wieseler and Tischendorf, construing the words with more latitude, put the Baptism *at the end* of our Lord's 31st year, and thus throw the whole ministry one year later.

on the Sabbath at Jerusalem, and thereby provokes the bitter hostility of the Sanhedrim.

The seventh chapter (in close connexion with this) begins by telling us that Jerusalem was no longer a safe place for Christ, that He could no longer 'walk in Jewry, because the Jews sought to kill Him;' and that therefore he remained in Galilee until the Feast of Tabernacles, when He once more appeared in the Temple. The way in which the controversy of the fifth chapter is resumed by our Lord, the way in which He speaks of the Sanhedrim's resolution to put Him to death, the way in which He alludes to His cure of the impotent man when He was last among them, as to something still fresh in men's minds, renders it highly improbable that the interval had been a long one.

'Why go ye about to kill Me?'

'I have done one work, and ye all marvel.'

'Are ye angry with Me because I have made a man every whit whole on the Sabbath-day?'

I cannot bring myself to believe that eighteen months had elapsed since the events which are thus alluded to. They are clearly alluded to as still in men's mouths, as still the subject of common talk in Jerusalem.

If this reasoning be accepted, and the interval be thus reduced from eighteen to six or seven months, then the whole Ministry is necessarily shortened from three years and a quarter to *two years and a quarter.*

In adopting this shorter term of the Ministry, it is satisfactory to have the support not only of Wieseler and those who follow him, but also of many of the early Fathers.

Jerome says plainly, 'It is written in St. John's

Gospel that our Lord attended three Passovers at Jerusalem, which make two complete years.'[1]

A still earlier writer, Irenæus, would seem in one place[2] to be of this opinion, resting it also on the fact that St. John distinctly implies *three Passovers,*—one soon after the miracle at Cana (ii. 13), one when Jesus 'cured the paralytic who for thirty-eight years had lain near the bath' (v. 1), and one, the final Passover, 'when He ate His paschal meal, and suffered on the following day' (xiii. 1).

With this, too, agrees the venerable tradition preserved by Eusebius[3], that when the Apostle John was an old man, the presbyters of Ephesus brought to him the three earlier Gospels, and that St. John approved them, and bore witness to their truth, only remarking that there was still wanting a record of the earlier portion of our Lord's ministry. And Eusebius adds, 'that this account is true, as any one may see; for those three Evangelists only relate the events of *that single year* which followed the Baptist's imprisonment, clearly indicating the same at the commencement of their narratives.'

These passages clearly testify an early belief in the Church that our Lord's ministry covered a space of little more than two complete years.

When Ignatius, Melito, Origen, and Chrysostom, in

---

[1] Jerome is commenting on the Greek version of Isaiah xxix. 1. 'Scriptum est in Evangelio secundum Joannem, per tria paschata Dominum venisse in Jerusalem, quæ duos annos efficiunt.'—*Op.* iii. 245.

[2] Iren. ii. 22, § 3.—The authority of this passage is, however, weakened by the curious inconsistency of the sequel, in which Irenæus seems to infer from John viii. 57, that the ministry lasted between ten and twenty years!

[3] *Eccles. Hist.* iii. 24.

the passages quoted by Greswell[1], speak of a 'three-years' ministry,' their language seems to me to agree better with the notion that the ministry was between *two and three* years, than with Greswell's notion that it was between *three and four*.

Indeed a two-and-a-quarter years' ministry would in Jewish phrase be certainly termed a 'three-years'' ministry,—just as Christ is said to have been *three night-days*[2] in the heart of the earth. And most naturally would Christ say, when visiting Jerusalem in the third spring of His Ministry, ' These three years I come seeking fruit on this fig-tree ' (Luke xiii. 7).

On all these grounds it may, I think, be safely concluded that the duration of our Lord's Ministry was *two years and a quarter*.

IV. *The unnamed feast of John* v. 1.—It will be observed that both Jerome and Irenæus, in the above-quoted passages, imply their conviction that this feast was a Passover ; and necessarily, therefore (as they only allow three Passovers), identify it with the Passover mentioned in John vi. 4. This identification seems to me perfectly possible, having regard to the close and intimate connexion of St. John's fifth and seventh chapters, and the quite independent character of the memoir (ch. vi.) which—possibly after the completion of his Gospel[3]—he inserted between them.

[1] Dissert. xiii. 2d ed.
[2] Matt. xii. 40. Our Lord used, no doubt, the Aramaic word corresponding to νυχθήμερα.
[3] It must strike every attentive reader that the opening words of the sixth chapter, ' After these things Jesus went over the sea of Galilee,' hardly suit the end of the fifth chapter, where our Lord was left in the Temple at Jerusalem ; nor yet do the opening words of the seventh chapter, giving a reason for leaving Jewry, suit the end of the sixth chapter, where our Lord was left at Capernaum ; whereas the begin-

But if this identification be judged impossible, then (with Wieseler and most moderns) we must fall back on Kepler's suggestion, that the unnamed feast was that of *Purim*, in the month preceding the Passover. The only important point is that the fifth and sixth chapters both belong to the spring of the same year, —the middle spring, as one may call it, of our Lord's ministry.

If the feast be Purim, our Lord must have gone up thus early to Jerusalem, meaning to stay there for the approaching Passover, but was obliged to leave prematurely by the outbreak of the Sanhedrim's hostility.

But four reasons dispose me to prefer the old Passover hypothesis to the modern one of Purim :—

1. None of the Fathers suggest Purim.

2. Not only the Paris Codex, but also the Sinaitic, have '*the* feast,' not '*a* feast.'

3. Our Lord at this feast (v. 35) seems to allude to the Baptist as to one recently dead, and we have reason to believe that the Baptist was murdered just before the Passover of A.D. 28[1].

4. The persecution of our Lord for allowing His disciples to rub the ears of corn seems to connect itself closely with this charge of Sabbath-breaking at the unnamed feast, and St. Luke's expression, that it ning of the seventh perfectly coheres with the end of the fifth chapter. I would venture, therefore, to suggest the possibility that the sixth chapter was added by St. John at the same time as the acknowledged postscript, chapter xxi. Both chapters, unlike the rest of the Gospel, are exclusively Galilean,—anecdotes of the Galilean Lake.

[1] It was at the γενέσια of Antipas ; and that these γενέσια were the anniversary not of his birthday, but of his accession (*i.e.* of the death of Herod the Great, p. 133) seems clear from Wieseler's quotations (p. 293), to which Plato, 1 *Alcib.* c. 17, may be added.

was 'on the *second-first* Sabbath,' points most probably to the *first* of the seven Sabbaths reckoned from the great *second* day of the Passover, before which it was unlawful to gather ears of corn[1]. Thus the incident is dated eight days after *a Passover*.

The much earlier mention of this rubbing of the ears by St. Mark and St. Luke is, no doubt, the grand difficulty which the theory of a two-and-a-quarter years' Ministry has to encounter. All we can say is that they were led to mention the rubbing of the ears and the healing of the withered hand thus prematurely in order to group them with those three earlier complaints of the Pharisees (the forgiveness of the Paralytic's sins, the eating with the Publicans, and the not-fasting of Christ's disciples). Not so St. Matthew. He separates by a long interval what St. Mark and St. Luke thus bring together.

V. *Date of the Crucifixion.*—Browne in his *Ordo Sæclorum* shows astronomically that in A.D. 29 the Paschal full moon fell on a Friday,—Friday 18th March ; and adopts this as the date of the Crucifixion[2]. Our Lord's age at His Baptism and the duration of His Ministry, as given above, point to this date also. It is satisfactory to remember that this year agrees with the constant tradition of the first five centuries (based doubtless on the *Acts of Pilate* before that document was corrupted), that Christ suffered in March in the Consulship of the Gemini, A.D. 29[3].

That our Lord suffered on a Friday is almost cer-

[1] Lev. xxiii. 14;—else why should St. Luke be careful to assign the date?
[2] Wieseler gives 7th April A.D. 30.
[3] See Tertull. *Adv. Jud.* viii. ; Aug. *De Civ. Dei*, xviii. 54, etc., and for the Consulship of the Gemini, see Tac. *Annal.* v. 1.

tain. But whether this Friday was the 14th or 15th of Nisan, is a question which has been much debated :—whether the Paschal lamb was slain on Good Friday, or on the preceding Thursday. On this question I must say a few words.

If we had the three earlier Evangelists only, no doubt could possibly have arisen : they clearly imply that the Passover was on the Thursday evening.

First we have our Lord's own words (Matt. xxvi. 1, 2) predicting that He would be betrayed at the Passover : ' Ye know that after two days is the Passover, and the Son of Man is betrayed to be crucified.' This is unintelligible unless the Passover was on the night of the betrayal,—the night *before* Good Friday. But still more explicit are St. Mark and St. Luke, who not only tell us that on the Thursday afternoon our Lord sent two of His Apostles to prepare the Paschal supper, but describe it most carefully as ' the first day of unleavened bread on which the Passover must be killed.' Words could not declare more clearly that the Passover, which our Lord said He had desired with so much desire to eat with His disciples before He suffered, was the regular Passover after the sunset of the 14th Nisan.

But before we dismiss the question we must turn to St. John, and show briefly that the four notes of time given in his Gospel agree with this.

1. Those for whom St. John wrote—unlike those for whom the three earlier Evangelists wrote—were familiar from childhood with the account of the institution of the Eucharist ; *that* therefore he omits ; but what the others had omitted, the account of the washing of the disciples' feet at that same supper, he gives in much detail. And how does he describe it ? He describes

it as taking place just before a meal, and that meal he tells us was the feast of the Passover (xiii. 1). 'Now before the Paschal feast, ... supper being on the table (for such is the right translation), ... Jesus rose and washed their feet.' Such is St. John's first note of time,—in perfect harmony, when read aright, with the earlier accounts.

2. Again, when Judas leaves the room, they think it is to buy something that they needed for the feast: —what feast? clearly the feast then going on; else why so much despatch?

3. Again, at six o'clock the next morning, St. John tells us the Pharisees would not enter the Roman hall lest they should be defiled, and so unable to eat their Passover.

It seems irregular, no doubt, that they should not have finished their Paschal lamb by six o'clock in the morning; but when one remembers how actively employed all night long in their wicked purposes these conspirators had been, there is no great difficulty in supposing that some portion of their Passover remained to be consumed.[1]

One more note of time there is in which St. John is so entirely in harmony with the other three that it seems strange that it should have occasioned difficulty. In common with all the Evangelists, St. John gives to Friday its ordinary Jewish name of ' Preparation-day.' Our translators, instead of saying, ' It was the preparation of the Passover,' should have rendered it simply ' It was the Friday of the Passover feast,' or, ' It was the Passover Friday.' Thus in all points it is easy to bring St. John's Gospel into harmony with the rest.

[1] Or Wieseler may be right in supposing that the phrase 'to eat the Passover' may have a wider meaning, as in 2 Chron. xxx. 22.

The Gospel Chronology.

		MATT.	MARK.	LUKE.	JOHN.
B.C. 5.					
March.	Annunciation, . . *Page* 18	...	...	1. 26	...
June.	Birth of Baptist, . . . 19	...	...	1. 57	...
Dec.	Birth of Jesus, ...	1. 21	...	2. 7	...
B.C. 4.					
Feb.	Presentation, ...	...	...	2. 22	...
	Wise men. Flight to Egypt, 20	2. 1	...	...	...
Apr.	Herod's death. Return, ...	2. 23	...	2. 39	...
A.D. 9.					
Mar. 29.	Passover; twelve years old, . 21	...	...	2. 42	...
A.D. 27.					
Feb.	Baptism. Temptation, . 24	3. 13	1. 9	3. 21	1. 32
Mar.	Miracle at Cana, . . . 26	...	...	...	2. 1
Apr. 9.	1st *Passover.* Clears Temple, 27	...	...	...	2. 13
	Ministry with the Baptist, . 28	...	...	...	3. 22
Dec.	Baptist imprisoned, . . 29	4. 12	1. 14	3. 20	...
	Journey through Samaria, ...	...	...	...	4. 4
A.D. 28.					
Jan.	Galilean ministry begins, . 30	4. 12	1. 15	4. 14	4. 43
	Nobleman's son healed, ...	...	...	...	4. 46
	Rejection at Nazareth, . 32	...	...	4. 16	...
	Makes Capernaum His home, 33	4. 13	...	4. 31	...
	Calls four Apostles, ...	4. 18	1. 16	5. 11*	...
	Peter's wife's mother cured, . 34	8. 14*	1. 29	4. 38	...
	1st Galilean tour, ...	4. 23	1. 39	4. 44	...
	Leper and Paralytic, ...	8. 2*	1. 40	5. 12	...
	Matthew called, ...	9. 9*	2. 14	5. 27	...
	The Twelve ordained, . . 34	10. 1*	3. 14	6. 12	...
	Sermon on Mount, . . 36	5, 6, 7	...	6. 20	...
	Centurion's servant cured, ...	8. 5	...	7. 1	...
	Widow's son raised at Nain, 35	...	...	7. 11	...
	Baptist's message, . . 36	11. 2*	...	7. 18	...
Feb.	2d Galilean tour with Twelve, ...	...	...	8. 1	...
	Parables, 'Sower,' etc., . 35	13. 1*	4. 1	8. 4	...
	Storm. Gadarene demoniac, ...	8. 28	5. 1	8. 26	...
	Jairus' daughter raised, ...	9. 18	5. 22	8. 41	...
March.	3d tour: the xii. two and two, ...	10. 1	6. 7	9. 1	...
	Baptist's death, . . . 37	14. 1	6. 14	9. 9	...
	5000 fed. Storm, . . 38	14. 15	6. 35	9. 12	6. 1*
Mar. 29.	2d *Passover.* Bethesda, . 40	...	...	...	5. 1

The Gospel Chronology. 143

			MATT.	MARK.	LUKE.	JOHN.
A.D. 28. Apr.	Pharisees' persecution, *Page*	41	15. 1	7. 1.	...	...
	Rubbing corn. Withered hand,	42	12. 1*	2. 23*	6. 1*	...
	Tyre, Sidon : the Canaanite, .	43	15. 21	7. 24	...	...
	Decapolis. 4000 fed, . .	44	15. 29	7. 31	...	...
	Prediction of death, . .	46	16. 16	8. 29	9. 20	...
Aug. (?)	Transfiguration, . . .	47	17. 1	9. 2	9. 28	...
Sep. 23.	Feast of Tabernacles, . .	50	...	...	...	7. 10
Nov. (?)	Farewell to Galilee, . .	52	19. 1	10. 1	9. 51	...
	Progress through Samaria, .	...	...	...	9. 52	...
	Mission of LXX., . . .	53	...	...	10. 1	...
	Martha and Mary (Bethany?) .	...	...	...	10. 38	...
	Controversy in Temple, . .	54	...	...	...	8. 12
	Sabbath cure of blind man, .	55	...	...	...	9. 1
Dec.	Feast of Dedication, . .	...	...	...	...	10. 22
A.D. 29. Jan.	Ministry beyond Jordan, .	56	19. 1	10. 1	...	10. 40
	(*Insert here Luke xi.-xviii.?*) .	57				
Feb. (?)	Raising of Lazarus, . .	58	...	...	...	11. 1
	Retirement to Ephraim, .	60	...	...	...	11. 54
March.	Ascending to Jerusalem, .	...	20. 17	10. 32	18. 31	...
	Jericho. Zaccheus, . .	61	20. 29	10. 46	18. 35	...
12.	*Sab.* Supper at Bethany, .	62	26. 6*	14. 3*	...	12. 2
13.	*Sun.* Messianic entry, . .	63	21. 1	11. 1	19. 29	12. 12
14.	*Mon.* Again clears Temple, .	65	21. 12	11. 15	19 45	...
15.	*Tues.* Controversy in Temple,	66	21. 23	11. 27	20. 1	...
16.	*Wed.* Interview with Greeks, .	70	...	...	...	12. 20
17.	*Thur.* 3d and last *Passover*, .	72	26. 17	14. 12	22. 7	13. 1
18.	*Fri.* Crucifixion, . . .	89	27. 1	15. 1	23. 1	19. 1
20.	*Sun.* Resurrection, . .	98	28. 1	16 1	24. 1	20. 1
	1st Appearance, to Mary, .	99	...	16. 9	...	20. 16
	2d, to the women, . .	100	28. 9	...	...	...
	3d, to Peter (1 Cor. xv. 5), .	101	...	...	24. 34	...
	4th, going to Emmaus, . .	102	...	16. 12	24. 15	...
	5th, in upper Chamber, . .	103	...	16. 14	24. 36	20. 19
27.	6th, *Sun.*, again in upper Chamber,	104	...	...	...	20. 26
April.	7th, to seven by the Lake, .	105	...	...	...	21. 1
	8th, to 500 at once (1 Cor. xv. 6),	106	28. 17	...	...	...
	9th, to James (1 Cor. xv. 7), .	107				
Ap. 28.	10th, to the Eleven. Ascension, ...		...	16. 19	24. 50	..

EDINBURGH : T. CONSTABLE,
PRINTER TO THE QUEEN, AND TO THE UNIVERSITY.

BY THE SAME AUTHOR.

In Crown 8vo, Price 5s,

"THE EDUCATION OF THE PEOPLE."

EDINBURGH: THOMAS LAURIE,
EDUCATIONAL PUBLISHER

October, 1869.

New Works

IN COURSE OF PUBLICATION

BY

MESSRS. RIVINGTON,

WATERLOO PLACE, LONDON;

HIGH STREET, OXFORD; TRINITY STREET, CAMBRIDGE.

The Origin and Development of Religious Belief.
By **S. Baring-Gould**, M.A., Author of "Curious Myths of the Middle Ages."
Part I. Heathenism and Mosaism.
8vo. 15*s.*

Brighstone Sermons.
Preached in the Parish Church of Brighstone, Isle of Wight.
By **George Moberly**, D.C.L., Bishop Designate of Sarum.
Crown 8vo. (*Just ready.*)

London, Oxford, and Cambridge

A

The First Book of Common Prayer

of Edward VI. and the Ordinal of 1549; together with the Order of the Communion, 1548.

Reprinted entire, and Edited by the Rev. **Henry Baskerville Walton**, M.A., late Fellow and Tutor of Merton College. With Introduction by the Rev. **Peter Goldsmith Medd**, M.A., Senior Fellow and Tutor of University College, Oxford.

Small 8vo. 6s.

A Manual for the Sick; with other

Devotions.

By **Lancelot Andrewes**, D.D., sometime Lord Bishop of Winchester.

Edited with a Preface by **H. P. Liddon**, M.A.

Large type. With Portrait. 24mo. 2s. 6d.

The Witness of St. Paul to Christ;

being the Boyle Lectures for 1869. With an Appendix, on the Credibility of the Acts, in Reply to the Recent Strictures of Dr. Davidson.

By the Rev. **Stanley Leathes**, M.A., Professor of Hebrew, King's College, London, and Preacher-Assistant, St. James's, Piccadilly.

8vo. 10s. 6d.

The Pursuit of Holiness:

a Sequel to "Thoughts on Personal Religion," intended to carry the Reader somewhat farther onward in the Spiritual Life.

By **Edward Meyrick Goulburn**, D.D., Dean of Norwich, and formerly one of Her Majesty's Chaplains in Ordinary.

Small 8vo. (*In the Press.*)

Apostolical Succession in the Church

of England.

By the Rev. **Arthur W. Haddan**, B.D., Rector of Barton-on-the-Heath, and late Fellow of Trinity College, Oxford.

8vo. 12s.

The Priest to the Altar; or, Aids to

the Devout Celebration of Holy Communion; chiefly after the Ancient Use of Sarum.

Second Edition. Enlarged, Revised, and Re-arranged with the Secretæ, Post-Communion, &c., appended to the Collects, Epistles, and Gospels, throughout the Year.

8vo. 7s. 6d.

The Reformation of the Church of

England; its History, Principles, and Results. A.D. 1514—1547. By **John Henry Blunt**, M.A., Vicar of Kennington, Oxford, Editor of "The Annotated Book of Common Prayer," Author of "Directorium Pastorale," &c., &c.

8vo. 16s.

Newman's (J. H.) Parochial and Plain

Sermons.

Edited by the Rev. **W. J. Copeland**, Rector of Farnham, Essex. From the Text of the last Editions published by Messrs. Rivington.

Complete in 8 Vols. Crown 8vo. 5s. each.

Newman's (J. H.) Sermons bearing upon

Subjects of the Day.

Edited by the Rev. **W. J. Copeland**, Rector of Farnham, Essex. From the Text of the last Edition published by Messrs. Rivington.

In One Volume. Crown 8vo. Printed uniformly with the "Parochial and Plain Sermons." 5s. (*Nearly ready.*)

The Pope and the Council.

By **Janus**. Authorized Translation from the German.

Crown 8vo. (*Just ready.*)

London, Oxford, and Cambridge

Sermons on the Characters of the Old Testament.

By the Rev. **Isaac Williams**, B.D., late Fellow of Trinity College, Oxford.

New Edition. Crown 8vo. 5s.

Female Characters of Holy Scripture.

In a Series of Sermons.

By the Rev. **Isaac Williams**, B.D., late of Trinity College, Oxford.

New Edition. Crown 8vo. 5s.

The Divinity of our Lord and Saviour

Jesus Christ; being the Bampton Lectures for 1866.

By **Henry Parry Liddon**, M.A., Student of Christ Church, and Chaplain to the Bishop of Salisbury.

Fourth Edition. Crown 8vo. 5s.

Sermons preached before the University

of Oxford.

By **Henry Parry Liddon**, M.A., Student of Christ Church, and Chaplain to the Bishop of Salisbury.

Third Edition, revised. Crown 8vo. 5s.

The Life of Madame Louise de France,

Daughter of Louis XV., also known as the Mother Térèse de S. Augustin. By the Author of "Tales of Kirkbeck."

Crown 8vo. 6s.

A Key to the Knowledge and Use of
the Book of Common Prayer.
By **John Henry Blunt**, M.A.
Small 8vo. 2s. 6d.

A Key to the Knowledge and Use of
the Holy Bible.
By **John Henry Blunt**, M.A.
Small 8vo. 2s. 6d.

A Key to the Knowledge of Church
History. (Ancient.)
Edited by **John Henry Blunt**, M.A.
Small 8vo. 2s. 6d.

A Key to the Narrative of the Four
Gospels.
By **John Pilkington Norris**, M.A., Canon of Bristol, formerly one of Her Majesty's Inspectors of Schools.
Small 8vo. 2s. 6d. (*Just ready.*)

The Story of the Gospels.
In a single Narrative, combined from the Four Evangelists, showing in a new translation their unity. To which is added a like continuous Narrative in the Original Greek.
By the Rev. **William Pound**, M.A., late Fellow of St. John's College, Cambridge, Principal of Appuldurcombe School, Isle of Wight.
In 2 Vols. 8vo. (*Nearly ready.*)

The Mysteries of Mount Calvary.
By **Antonio de Guevara**.
Forming the Lent Volume of the "Ascetic Library," a Series of Translations of Spiritual Works for Devotional Reading from Catholic Sources. Edited by the Rev. **Orby Shipley**, M.A.
Square Crown 8vo. 3s. 6d.

Preparation for Death.
Translated from the Italian of Alfonso, Bishop of S. Agatha. Forming the Advent Volume of the "Ascetic Library," a Series of Translations of Spiritual Works for Devotional Reading from Catholic Sources. Edited by the Rev. **Orby Shipley**, M.A.
Square Crown 8vo. 5s.

Counsels on Holiness of Life.
Translated from the Spanish of "The Sinner's Guide" by **Luis de Granada**. Forming a volume of the "Ascetic Library," a Series of Translations of Spiritual Works for Devotional Reading from Catholic Sources. Edited by the Rev. **Orby Shipley**, M.A.
Square Crown 8vo. 5s.

Examination of Conscience upon Special
Subjects. Translated and abridged from the French of **Tronson**. Forming a volume of the "Ascetic Library," a Series of Translations of Spiritual Works for Devotional Reading from Catholic Sources. Edited by the Rev. **Orby Shipley**, M.A.
Square Crown 8vo. (*In the Press.*)

The Manor Farm: a Tale.
By the Author of "The Hillford Confirmation."
Small 8vo. With Illustrations. (*In the Press.*)

The Virgin's Lamp:
Prayers and Devout Exercises for English Sisters, chiefly composed and selected by the late Rev. J. M. Neale, D.D., Founder of St. Margaret's, East Grinstead.
Small 8vo. 3s. 6d.

Catechetical Notes and Class Questions,
Literal and Mystical; chiefly on the Earlier Books of Holy Scripture.
By the late Rev. J. M. Neale, D.D., Warden of Sackville College, East Grinstead.
Crown 8vo. 5s.

Sermons for Children; being Thirty-
three short Readings, addressed to the Children of S. Margaret's Home, East Grinstead.
By the late Rev. J. M. Neale, D.D., Warden of Sackville College.
Second Edition. Small 8vo. 3s. 6d.

Sketches of the Rites and Customs of
the Greco-Russian Church.
By H. C. Romanoff. With an Introductory Notice by the Author of "The Heir of Redclyffe."
Second Edition. Crown 8vo. 7s. 6d.

The Treasury of Devotion: a Manual
of Prayers for general and daily use.
Compiled by a Priest. Edited by the Rev. T. T. Carter, Rector of Clewer.
16mo, limp cloth, 2s.; cloth, 2s. 6d.
Bound with the Book of Common Prayer. Cloth. 3s. 6d.

The Witness of the Old Testament to
Christ. The Boyle Lectures for the Year 1868.
By the Rev. Stanley Leathes, M.A., Preacher at St. James's, Westminster, and Professor of Hebrew in King's College, London.
8vo. 9s.

London, Oxford, and Cambridge

Liber Precum Publicarum Ecclesiæ

Anglicanæ.
À **Gulielmo Bright,** A.M., et **Petro Goldsmith Medd,** A.M., Presbyteris, Collegii Universitatis in Acad. Oxon. Sociis, Latine redditus.

In an elegant pocket volume, with all the Rubrics in red.

New Edition. Small 8vo. 6s.

Bible Readings for Family Prayer.

By the Rev. **W. H. Ridley,** M.A., Rector of Hambleden.
Old Testament—Genesis and Exodus.
New Testament { St. Luke and St. John.
{ St. Matthew and St. Mark. *(In the Press.)*

Crown 8vo. 2s. each.

Miscellaneous Poems.

By **Henry Francis Lyte,** M.A.

New Edition. Small 8vo. 5s.

Devotional Commentary on the Gospel

according to S. Matthew.
Translated from the French of **Pasquier Quesnel.**

Crown 8vo. 7s. 6d.

Sermons on Doctrines. For the Middle

Classes. By the Rev. **George Wray,** M.A., Prebendary of York, and Rector of Leven, near Beverley.

Small 8vo. 5s. 6d.

Eirenicon, Part II. A Letter to the

Very Rev. J. H. Newman, D.D., in Explanation chiefly in regard to the Reverential Love due to the ever-blessed Theotokos, and the Doctrine of her Immaculate Conception; with an Analysis of Card. de Turrecremata's Work on the Immaculate Conception. By the Rev. E. B. Pusey, D.D., Regius Professor of Hebrew, and Canon of Christ Church.

8vo. 7s. 6d.

The Sufferings of Jesus.

Composed by Fra Thomé de Jesu, of the Order of Hermits of S. Augustine, a Captive of Barbary, in the Fiftieth year of his Banishment from Heaven. Translated from the original Portuguese.

Part I. Our Lord's Sufferings, from the hour of His Conception to the night of His Betrayal.

Part II. Our Lord's Sufferings, from the Agony in the Garden to His Death.

Edited by the Rev. E. B. Pusey, D.D.

Two Volumes, small 8vo. 7s.

Daniel the Prophet: Nine Lectures

delivered in the Divinity School of the University of Oxford. With copious Notes. By the Rev. E. B. Pusey, D.D., Regius Professor of Hebrew, and Canon of Christ Church.

Second Edition. 8vo. 10s. 6d.

Eleven Addresses during a Retreat of

the Companions of the Love of Jesus, engaged in Perpetual Intercession for the Conversion of Sinners. By the Rev. E. B. Pusey, D.D., Regius Professor of Hebrew, and Canon of Christ Church.

8vo. 3s. 6d.

London, Oxford, and Cambridge

Spiritual Life.
By **John James**, D.D., late Canon of Peterborough, Author of a "Comment on the Collects of the Church of England," &c.

12mo. 5s.

Professor Inman's Nautical Tables,
for the use of British Seamen. *New Edition*, by the Rev. **J. W. Inman**, late Fellow of St. John's College, Cambridge, and Head Master of Chudleigh Grammar School. Revised, and enlarged by the introduction of Tables of ½ log. haversines, log. differences, &c.; with a more compendious method of Working a Lunar, and a Catalogue of Latitudes and Longitudes of Places on the Seaboard.

Royal 8vo. 16s.

The Doctrine of the Church of England,
as stated in Ecclesiastical Documents set forth by Authority of Church and State, in the Reformation Period between 1536 and 1662. Edited by the Rev. **John Henry Blunt**, M.A.

8vo. 7s. 6d.

Annals of the Bodleian Library, Oxford,
from its Foundation to A.D. 1867; containing an Account of the various collections of printed books and MSS. there preserved; with a brief Preliminary Sketch of the earlier Library of the University.

By **W. D. Macray**, M.A., Assistant in the Library, Chaplain of Magdalen and New Colleges.

8vo. 12s.

England versus Rome: a Brief Handbook
of the Roman Catholic Controversy, for the use of Members of the English Church.

By **Henry Barclay Swete**, M.A., Fellow of Gonville and Caius College, Cambridge.

16mo. 2s. 6d.

Thomas à Kempis, Of the Imitation of Christ.

A carefully revised translation, elegantly printed with red borders.
16mo. 2s. 6d.
Also a cheap Edition, without the red borders, 1s., or in Cover, 6d.

The Rule and Exercises of Holy Living.

By **Jeremy Taylor**, D.D., Bishop of Down, and Connor, and Dromore.
A New Edition, elegantly printed with red borders.
16mo. 2s. 6d.
Also a cheap Edition, without the red borders, 1s.

The Rule and Exercises of Holy Dying.

By **Jeremy Taylor**, D.D., Bishop of Down, and Connor, and Dromore.
A New Edition, elegantly printed with red borders.
16mo. 2s. 6d.
Also a cheap Edition, without the red borders, 1s.

*** The Holy Living and Holy Dying may be had bound together in One Volume. 5s., or without the red borders, 2s. 6d.

A Short and Plain Instruction for the

better Understanding of the Lord's Supper; to which is annexed, the Office of the Holy Communion, with proper Helps and Directions.

By **Thomas Wilson**, D.D., late Lord Bishop of Sodor and Man.

New and complete Edition, elegantly printed in large type, with rubrics and borders in red. 16mo. 2s. 6d.
Also a cheap Edition, without the red borders, 1s., or in Cover, 6d.

Introduction to the Devout Life.

From the French of Saint Francis of Sales, Bishop and Prince of Geneva.
A New Translation, elegantly printed with red borders.
16mo. 2s. 6d.

London, Oxford, and Cambridge

Vestiarivm Christianvm: the Origin

and Gradual Development of the Dress of the Holy Ministry in the Church, as evidenced by Monuments both of Literature and of Art, from the Apostolic Age to the present time.

By the Rev. **Wharton B. Marriott**, M.A., F.S.A. (sometime Fellow of Exeter College, Oxford, and Assistant-Master at Eton), Select Preacher in the University, and Preacher, by licence from the Bishop, in the Diocese of Oxford.
Royal 8vo. 38s.

The Annotated Book of Common

Prayer; being an Historical, Ritual, and Theological Commentary on the Devotional System of the Church of England.
Edited by **John Henry Blunt**, M.A.
Fourth Edition. Imperial 8vo. 36s.

The Prayer Book Interleaved;

with Historical Illustrations and Explanatory Notes arranged parallel to the Text, by the Rev. **W. M. Campion**, B.D., Fellow and Tutor of Queens' College and Rector of St. Botolph's, and the Rev. **W. J. Beamont**, M.A., late Fellow of Trinity College, Cambridge, and Incumbent of St. Michael's, Cambridge. With a Preface by the **Lord Bishop of Ely**.
Fourth Edition. Small 8vo. 7s. 6d.

Flowers and Festivals; or, Directions

for the Floral Decorations of Churches. With coloured Illustrations.

By **W. A. Barrett**, of S. Paul's Cathedral, late Clerk of Magdalen College, and Commoner of S. Mary Hall, Oxford.
Square Crown 8vo. 5s.

Light in the Heart; or, Short Medita-
tions on Subjects which concern the Soul. Translated from the French.
Edited by the Rev. **W. J. Butler**, M.A., Vicar of Wantage.
Small 8vo. 1s. 6d.

The True Passover.
By **Thomas Parry**, D.D., Bishop of Barbados.
Small 8vo. 1s. 6d.

Sickness; its Trials and Blessings.
Fine Edition, on toned paper. Small 8vo. 3s. 6d.
Also, a Cheap Edition, 1s. 6d., or in Paper Cover, 1s.

Help and Comfort for the Sick Poor.
By the Author of "Sickness; its Trials and Blessings."
New Edition. Small 8vo. 1s.

Hymns and Poems for the Sick and
Suffering; in connexion with the Service for the Visitation of the Sick. Selected from various Authors.
Edited by **T. V. Fosbery**, M.A., Vicar of St. Giles's, Reading.
New and cheaper Edition. Small 8vo. 3s. 6d.

The Dogmatic Faith: an Inquiry
into the Relation subsisting between Revelation and Dogma. Being the Bampton Lectures for 1867.
By **Edward Garbett**, M.A., Incumbent of Christ Church, Surbiton.
Second Edition. Crown 8vo. 5s.

London, Oxford, and Cambridge

Dean Alford's Greek Testament.

With English Notes, intended for the Upper Forms of Schools, and for Pass-men at the Universities. Abridged by **Bradley H. Alford**, M.A., Vicar of Leavenheath, Colchester; late Scholar of Trinity College, Cambridge.
Crown 8vo. 10s. 6d.

Household Theology: a Handbook of

Religious Information respecting the Holy Bible, the Prayer Book, the Church, the Ministry, Divine Worship, the Creeds, &c. &c.
By **John Henry Blunt**, M.A.
Third Edition. Small 8vo. 3s. 6d.

Curious Myths of the Middle Ages.

By **S. Baring-Gould**, M.A., Author of "Post-Mediæval Preachers," &c. With Illustrations.
New Edition. Complete in one Volume.
Crown 8vo. 6s.

Soimême: a Story of a Wilful Life.

Small 8vo. 3s. 6d.

Miss Langley's Will: a Tale.

Second Edition. 2 Vols. Post 8vo. £1 1s.

The History of the Church of Ireland.
In Eight Sermons preached in Westminster Abbey.
By Chr. Wordsworth, D.D., Bishop of Lincoln, formerly Canon of Westminster and Archdeacon.
Crown 8vo. 6s.

The Holy Bible.
With Notes and Introductions.
By Chr. Wordsworth, D.D., Bishop of Lincoln, formerly Canon of Westminster, and Archdeacon.
Imperial 8vo.

Part		£ s. d.
Vol. I. 38s.	I. Genesis and Exodus. *Second Edit.*	1 1 0
	II. Leviticus, Numbers, Deuteronomy. *Second Edition*	0 18 0
Vol. II. 21s.	III. Joshua, Judges, Ruth. *Second Edit.*	0 12 0
	IV. The Books of Samuel. *Second Edit.*	0 10 0
Vol. III. 21s.	V. The Books of Kings, Chronicles, Ezra, Nehemiah, Esther. *Second Edition*	1 1 0
Vol. IV. 34s.	VI. The Book of Job. *Second Edition*	0 9 0
	VII. The Book of Psalms. *Second Edit.*	0 15 0
	VIII. Proverbs, Ecclesiastes, Song of Solomon	0 12 0
Vol. V.	IX. Isaiah	0 12 6
	X. Jeremiah, Lamentations, and Ezekiel	1 1 0
	XI. The Minor Prophets. (*In Preparation.*)	

Manual of Family Devotions, arranged
from the Book of Common Prayer.
By the Hon. Augustus Duncombe, D.D., Dean of York.
Printed in red and black.
Small 8vo. 3s. 6d.

Anglo-Saxon Witness on Four Alleged

Requisites for Holy Communion—Fasting, Water, Altar Lights, and Incense.
By Rev. **J. Baron**, M.A. Rector of Upton Scudamore, Wilts.

8vo. 5s.

Perranzabuloe, the Lost Church Found;

or, The Church of England not a New Church, but Ancient, Apostolical, and Independent, and a Protesting Church Nine Hundred Years before the Reformation.
By the Rev. **C. T. Collins Trelawny**, M.A., formerly Rector of Timsbury, Somerset, and late Fellow of Balliol College, Oxford. With Illustrations.

New Edition. Crown 8vo. 3s. 6d.

The Sacraments and Sacramental Or-

dinances of the Church; being a Plain Exposition of their History, Meaning, and Effects.
By **John Henry Blunt**, M.A.

Small 8vo. 4s. 6d.

Catechesis; or, Christian Instruction

preparatory to Confirmation and First Communion.
By the Rev. **Charles Wordsworth**, D.C.L., Bishop of St. Andrew's.

New and cheaper Edition. Small 8vo. 2s.

Village Sermons on the Baptismal

Service.
By the Rev. **John Keble**, Author of "The Christian Year."

8vo. 5s.

London, Oxford, and Cambridge

Warnings of the Holy Week, &c.;

being a Course of Parochial Lectures for the Week before Easter and the Easter Festivals.
By the Rev. **W. Adams**, M.A., late Vicar of St. Peter's-in-the-East, Oxford, and Fellow of Merton College.
Sixth Edition. Small 8vo. 4s. 6d.

A Glossary of Ecclesiastical Terms;

containing Explanations of Terms used in Architecture, Ecclesiology, Hymnology, Law, Ritualism, Theology, Heresies, and Miscellaneous Subjects.
By Various Writers. Edited by the Rev. **Orby Shipley**, M.A.
Crown 8vo. (*In the Press.*)

An Illuminated Edition of the Book of

Common Prayer, printed in Red and Black, on fine toned Paper; with Borders and Titles, designed after the manner of the 14th Century, by **R. R. Holmes**, F.S.A., and engraved by **O. Jewitt**.
Crown 8vo. White vellum cloth illuminated. 16s.

This Edition of the PRAYER BOOK *may be had in various Bindings for presentation.*

Yesterday, To-day, and For Ever: a

Poem in Twelve Books.
By **Edward Henry Bickersteth**, M.A., Incumbent of Christ Church, Hampstead, and Chaplain to the Bishop of Ripon.
Third Edition. Small 8vo. 6s.

The Hillford Confirmation: a Tale.

By **M. C. Phillpotts**.
18mo. 1s.

London, Oxford, and Cambridge

B

The Greek Testament.
With Notes and Introductions.
By **Chr. Wordsworth**, D.D., Bishop of Lincoln; formerly Canon of Westminster, and Archdeacon.
2 Vols. Impl. 8vo. 4*l*.
The Parts may be had separately, as follows:—
The Gospels, 6*th Edition*, 21*s*.
The Acts, 5*th Edition*, 10*s*. 6*d*.
St. Paul's Epistles, 5*th Edition*, 31*s*. 6*d*.
General Epistles, Revelation, and Indexes, 3*rd Edition*, 21*s*.

Occasional Sermons.
By **Henry Parry Liddon**, M.A., Student of Christ Church, and Chaplain to the Bishop of Salisbury.
Crown 8vo. (*In Preparation.*)

From Morning to Evening:
a Book for Invalids.
From the French of M. L'Abbé Henri Perreyve. Translated and adapted by an Associate of the Sisterhood of S. John Baptist, Clewer.
Crown 8vo. 5*s*.

Popular Objections to the Book of
Common Prayer considered, in Four Sermons on the Sunday Lessons in Lent, the Commination Service, and the Athanasian Creed, with a Preface on the existing Lectionary.
By **Edward Meyrick Goulburn**, D.D., Dean of Norwich.
Second Edition. Small 8vo. 2*s*. 6*d*.

Family Prayers: compiled from various
sources (chiefly from Bishop Hamilton's Manual), and arranged on the Liturgical Principle.
By **Edward Meyrick Goulburn**, D.D., Dean of Norwich.
New Edition. Crown 8vo, large type, 3*s*. 6*d*.
Cheap Edition. 16mo. 1*s*.

The Annual Register: a Review of
Public Events at Home and Abroad, for the Year 1868; being the Sixth Volume of an improved Series.

8vo. 18s.

⁎ *The Volumes for 1863 to 1867 may be had, price* 18s. *each.*

Arithmetic, Theoretical and Practical;
adapted for the use of Colleges and Schools.

By **W. H. Girdlestone**, M.A., of Christ's College, Cambridge.

New and Revised Edition. Crown 8vo. (*Just ready.*)

Egypt's Record of Time to the Exodus
of Israel, critically investigated : with a comparative Survey of the Patriarchal History and the Chronology of Scripture; resulting in the Reconciliation of the Septuagint and Hebrew Computations, and Manetho with both.

By **W. B. Galloway**, M.A., Vicar of St. Mark's, Regent's Park, and Chaplain to the Right Hon. Lord Viscount Hawarden.

8vo. 15s.

A Fourth Series of Parochial Sermons,
preached in a Village Church.

By the Rev. **Charles A. Heurtley**, D.D., Rector of Fenny Compton, Warwickshire, Margaret Professor of Divinity, and Canon of Christ Church, Oxford.

12mo. 5s. 6d.

Six Short Sermons on Sin. Lent Lectures
at S. Alban the Martyr, Holborn.

By the Rev. **Orby Shipley**, M.A.

Fourth Edition. Small 8vo. 1s.

London, Oxford, and Cambridge

Vox Ecclesiæ Anglicanæ : on the
Church Ministry and Sacraments. A Selection of Passages from the Writings of the Chief Divines of the Church of England. With short Introductions and Notices of the Writers.

By **George G. Perry**, M.A., Prebendary of Lincoln, Rector of Waddington, Rural Dean, and Proctor for the Diocese of Lincoln.

Crown 8vo. 6s.

Reflections on the Revolution in France,
and on the Proceedings in certain Societies in London relative to that Event. In a Letter intended to have been sent to a Gentleman in Paris, 1790.

By the Right Hon. **Edmund Burke**, M.P.

New Edition. With a short Biographical Notice.

Crown 8vo. 3s. 6d.

A Memoir of the late Henry Hoare,
Esq., M.A. With a Narrative of the Church Movements with which he was connected from 1848 to 1865.

By **James Bradby Sweet**, M.A., Stipendiary Curate of Colkirk.

8vo. (*In the Press.*)

Aids to Prayer: a Course of Lectures
delivered at Holy Trinity Church, Paddington.

By **Daniel Moore**, M.A., Honorary Chaplain to the Queen, &c.

Crown 8vo. 4s. 6d.

The Perfect Man; or, Jesus an Example
of Godly Life.

By the Rev. **Harry Jones**, M.A., Incumbent of St. Luke's, Berwick Street.

Crown 8vo. 3s. 6d.

London, Oxford, and Cambridge

A Practical Treatise concerning Evil

Thoughts: wherein their Nature, Origin, and Effect are distinctly considered and explained, with many Useful Rules for restraining and suppressing such Thoughts: suited to the various conditions of Life, and the several Tempers of Mankind, more especially of melancholy Persons.
By **William Chilcot**, M.A.
With Preface and Notes by **Richard Hooper**, M.A., Vicar of Upton and Aston Upthorpe, Berks.
Third Edition, elegantly printed with red borders.
16mo. 2s. 6d.

Sacred Allegories:

The Shadow of the Cross—The Distant Hills—The Old Man's Home—The King's Messengers.
By the Rev. **W. Adams**, M.A., late Fellow of Merton College, Oxford.
New Edition. Illustrated. Small 4to. 10s. 6d. (*Nearly ready.*)

Selections from Modern French Authors.

With English Notes and Introductory Notice.
By **Henri Van Laun**, French Master at Cheltenham College.
Part 1.—Honoré de Balzac.
Crown 8vo. 3s. 6d.

A Course of Lectures delivered to Candidates for Holy Orders,

comprising a Summary of the whole System of Theology. To which is prefixed an Inaugural Address.
By **John Randolph**, D.D. (sometime Bishop of London).
Vol. I. Natural and Revealed. 7s. 6d.
Vol. II. Historical. } (*In the Press.*)
Vol. III. Doctrinal. }
In 3 Vols. 8vo.

London, Oxford, and Cambridge

Farewell Counsels of a Pastor to his

Flock, on the Topics of the Day. Nine Sermons preached at St. John's, Paddington.
Third Edition. Small 8vo. 4s.

The Greek Testament.

With a Critically revised Text; a Digest of Various Readings; Marginal References to Verbal and Idiomatic Usage; Prolegomena; and a Critical and Exegetical Commentary. For the use of Theological Students and Ministers. By **Henry Alford**, D.D., Dean of Canterbury.
4 Vols. 8vo. 102s.

The Volumes are sold separately as follows :—
Vol. I.—The Four Gospels. *Sixth Edition.* 28s.
Vol. II.—Acts to II. Corinthians. *Fifth Edition.* 24s.
Vol. III.—Galatians to Philemon. *Fourth Edition.* 18s.
Vol. IV.—Hebrews to Revelation. *Third Edition.* 32s.

The New Testament for English

Readers; containing the Authorized Version, with a revised English Text; Marginal References; and a Critical and Explanatory Commentary. By **Henry Alford**, D.D., Dean of Canterbury.

Now complete in 2 Vols. or 4 Parts, price 54s. 6d.

Separately,
Vol. 1, Part I.—The three first Gospels, with a Map. *Second Edition.* 12s.
Vol. 1, Part II.—St. John and the Acts. *Second Edition.* 10s. 6d.
Vol. 2, Part I.—The Epistles of St. Paul, with a Map. *Second Edition.* 16s.
Vol. 2, Part II.—Hebrews to Revelation. 8vo. 16s.

The Sword and the Keys.

The Civil Power in its Relations to The Church; considered with Special Reference to the Court of Final Ecclesiastical Appeal in England. With Appendix containing all Statutes on which the Jurisdiction of that Tribunal over Spiritual Causes is Founded, and also, all Ecclesiastical Judgments delivered by it since those published by the Lord Bishop of London in 1865. By **James Wayland Joyce**, M.A., Rector of Burford, Salop. 8vo. 10s. 6d.

An Attempt to determine John Wes-

ley's place in Church History, with the aid of Facts and Documents unknown to, or unnoticed by, his Biographers. By **R. Denny-Urlin**, M.R.I.A., of the Middle Temple, Barrister-at-Law; Author of "The Office of Trustee," &c., &c. Small 8vo. (*In the Press.*)

Consoling Thoughts in Sickness.

Edited by **Henry Bailey**, B.D., Warden of St. Augustine's College, Canterbury.
Large type. Small 8vo. 2s. 6d.

Thoughts on Personal Religion; being

a Treatise on the Christian Life in its Two Chief Elements, Devotion and Practice.
By **Edward Meyrick Goulburn**, D.D., Dean of Norwich.
New Edition. Small 8vo. 6s. 6d.
An Edition for Presentation, Two Volumes, small 8vo. 10s. 6d.
Also, a Cheap Edition. Small 8vo. 3s. 6d.

On Miracles; being the Bampton

Lectures for 1865.
By **J. B Mozley**, B.D., Canon of Worcester, late Fellow of Magdalen College, Oxford.
Second Edition. 8vo. 10s. 6d.

London, Oxford, and Cambridge

Nearly ready, in Imperial 8vo.

PART I. (CONTAINING A—I.)

A DICTIONARY OF DOCTRINAL AND HISTORICAL THEOLOGY,

BY VARIOUS WRITERS.

EDITED BY THE

REV. JOHN HENRY BLUNT, M.A., F.S.A.,

EDITOR OF "THE ANNOTATED BOOK OF COMMON PRAYER."

THIS is the first portion of the " Summary of Theology and Ecclesiastical History," which Messrs. Rivington propose to publish in eight volumes as a " Thesaurus Theologicus" for the Clergy and Reading Laity of the Church of England.

It consists of original articles on all the important Doctrines of Theology, and on other questions necessary for their further illustration, the articles being carefully written with a view to modern thought, as well as a respect for ancient authority.

The Dictionary will be completed in two parts.

London, Oxford, and Cambridge

NEW PAMPHLETS

BY THE BISHOP OF ST. DAVID'S.

The Spirit of Truth the Holy Spirit: a Sermon,
preached before the University of Cambridge, on Whitsunday, May 16, 1869.
8vo. 1s.

BY ARCHDEACON BICKERSTETH.

Christian Mourners not Hopeless Mourners: a
Sermon, preached in the Parish Church of Monks' Risborough, on Sunday,
June 27, 1869, on the occasion of the Death of Mrs. Evetts, wife of the Rector
of that parish. 8vo. 1s.

The Filling of all Things by our Ascended Lord: a
Sermon, preached in Westminster Abbey, on St. Matthias' Day, Feb. 24,
1869, on the Occasion of the Consecration of Dr. Wordsworth, Bishop Elect
of Lincoln; Dr. Hatchard, Bishop Designate of Mauritius; and Dr. Turner,
Bishop Designate of Grafton and Armidale. 8vo. 1s.

BY THE REV. H. P. LIDDON.

Life in Death: a Sermon, preached in Salisbury
Cathedral, on the 11th Sunday after Trinity, August 8, 1869, being the day
after the Funeral of Walter Kerr Hamilton, D.D., Lord Bishop of Salisbury.
8vo. 1s.

A Sister's Work: a Sermon, preached in substance
at All Saints', Margaret Street, on the Second Sunday after Trinity, 1869.
8vo. 1s.

Christ and Human Law: a Sermon, preached before the University, the Hon. Mr. Justice Hannen, and the Hon. Mr. Justice
Keating, Her Majesty's learned Judges of Assize, in the Church of St. Mary
the Virgin, Oxford, on the Third Sunday in Lent, February 28, 1869. *Second
Edition.* With a Note on Divorce. 8vo. 1s.

Christ and Education: a Sermon, preached at St.
James's, Piccadilly, on the Third Sunday after Trinity, 1869. 8vo. 1s.

London, Oxford, and Cambridge

NEW PAMPHLETS

BY THE REV. R. W. BARNES.

Three Sermons, preached in Exeter Cathedral, on the
7th, 8th, and 9th Sundays after Trinity, July 11th, 18th, and 25th, 1869. 8vo. 1s. 6d.

BY THE REV. C. N. GRAY.

Statement on Confession. With full Catena of
Anglican Divines. *Third Edition.* 6d.

BY THE REV. JAMES GERALD JOYCE.

Can the Liturgy be used to attach the People to the
Church? A Paper, read before the Churchman's Association for the Rural Deaneries of Andover, Basingstoke, and Chilbolton. 8vo. 1s.

BY THE REV. GEORGE HENRY SUMNER.

Peace, Christ's Legacy to His Church: a Sermon
preached in Westminster Abbey, at the Consecration of the Rev. Ashton Oxenden, D.D., to the Metropolitan See of Montreal, on Sunday, August 1, 1869. 8vo. 1s.

BY THE REV. G. I. PELLEW.

A Sermon, preached at St. Mary's Church, Putney,
in the Defence of the Athanasian Creed, on the first Sunday after Trinity, 1869. 8vo. 6d.

A Review of Mariolatry, Liturgical, Devotional,
Doctrinal, as exhibited in the Offices, the Devotional and Dogmatic Books, at present used in the Romish Communion. 8vo. 1s. 6d.

The Reformation of the Church of England.
[A.D. 1514—1547.] A Review, Reprinted by Permission from the "Times," of February 27th and March 1st, 1869. 8vo. 6d.

London, Oxford, and Cambridge

CATENA CLASSICORUM,
A SERIES OF CLASSICAL AUTHORS,
EDITED BY MEMBERS OF BOTH UNIVERSITIES UNDER
THE DIRECTION OF

THE REV. ARTHUR HOLMES, M.A.
FELLOW AND LECTURER OF CLARE COLLEGE, CAMBRIDGE, LECTURER AND LATE
FELLOW OF ST. JOHN'S COLLEGE,

AND

THE REV. CHARLES BIGG, M.A.
LATE SENIOR STUDENT AND TUTOR OF CHRIST CHURCH, OXFORD, SECOND
CLASSICAL MASTER OF CHELTENHAM COLLEGE.

The following Parts have been already published:—

SOPHOCLIS TRAGOEDIAE,
Edited by R. C. JEBB, M.A. Fellow and Assistant Tutor of Trinity
College, Cambridge.
 [Part I. The Electra. 3s. 6d. Part II. The Ajax. 3s. 6d.

JUVENALIS SATIRAE,
Edited by G. A. SIMCOX, M.A. Fellow and Classical Lecturer of
Queen's College, Oxford. [Thirteen Satires. 3s. 6d.

THUCYDIDIS HISTORIA,
Edited by CHARLES BIGG, M.A. late Senior Student and Tutor of
Christ Church, Oxford. Second Classical Master of Cheltenham College.
 [Vol. I. Books I. and II. with Introductions. 6s.

DEMOSTHENIS ORATIONES PUBLICAE,
Edited by G. H. HESLOP, M.A. late Fellow and Assistant Tutor
of Queen's College, Oxford. Head Master of St. Bees.
 [Parts I. & II. The Olynthiacs and the Philippics. 4s. 6d.

ARISTOPHANIS COMOEDIAE,
Edited by W. C. GREEN, M.A. late Fellow of King's College,
Cambridge. Classical Lecturer at Queens' College.
 [Part I. The Acharnians and the Knights. 4s.
 [Part II. The Clouds. 3s. 6d.
 [Part III. The Wasps. 3s. 6d.

ISOCRATIS ORATIONES,
Edited by JOHN EDWIN SANDYS, B.A. Fellow and Lecturer of
St. John's College, and Lecturer at Jesus College, Cambridge.
 [Part I. Ad Demonicum et Panegyricus. 4s. 6d.

A PERSII FLACCI SATIRARUM LIBER,
Edited by A. PRETOR, M.A., of Trinity College, Cambridge,
Classical Lecturer of Trinity Hall. 3s. 6d.

London, Oxford, and Cambridge

CATENA CLASSICORUM—Opinions of the Press.

Mr. Jebb's Sophocles.

"Of Mr. Jebb's scholarly edition of the 'Electra' of Sophocles we cannot speak too highly. The whole Play bears evidence of the taste, learning, and fine scholarship of its able editor. Illustrations drawn from the literature of the Continent as well as of England, and the researches of the highest classical authorities are embodied in the notes, which are brief, clear, and always to the point."—*London Review, March 16, 1867.*

"The editorship of the work before us is of a very high order, displaying at once ripe scholarship, sound judgment, and conscientious care. An excellent Introduction gives an account of the various forms assumed in Greek literature by the legend upon which 'The Electra' is founded, and institutes a comparison between it and the 'Choephorae' of Æschylus. The text is mainly that of Dindorf. In the notes, which are admirable in every respect, is to be found exactly what is wanted, and yet they rather suggest and direct further inquiry than supersede exertion on the part of the student."—*Athenæum.*

"The Introduction proves that Mr. Jebb is something more than a mere scholar,—a man of real taste and feeling. His criticism upon Schlegel's remarks on the Electra are, we believe, new, and certainly just. As we have often had occasion to say in this Review, it is impossible to pass any reliable criticism upon school-books until they have been tested by experience. The notes, however, in this case appear to be clear and sensible, and direct attention to the points where attention is most needed."—*Westminster Review.*

"We have no hesitation in saying that in style and manner Mr. Jebb's notes are admirably suited for their purpose. The explanations of grammatical points are singularly lucid, the parallel passages generally well chosen, the translations bright and graceful, the analysis of arguments terse and luminous. Mr. Jebb has clearly shown that he possesses some of the qualities most essential for a commentator."—*Spectator.*

"The notes appear to us exactly suited to assist boys of the Upper Forms at Schools, and University students; they give sufficient help without over-doing explanations. . . . His critical remarks show acute and exact scholarship, and a very useful addition to ordinary notes is the scheme of metres in the choruses."—*Guardian.*

"If, as we are fain to believe, the editors of the *Catena Classicorum* have got together such a pick of scholars as have no need to play their best card first, there is a bright promise of success to their series in the first sample of it which has come to hand —Mr. Jebb's 'Electra.' We have seen it suggested that it is unsafe to pronounce on the merits of a Greek Play edited for educational purposes until it has been tested in the hands of pupils and tutors. But our examination of the instalment of, we hope, a complete 'Sophocles,' which Mr. Jebb has put forth, has assured us that this is a needless suspension of judgment, and prompted us to commit the justifiable rashness of pronouncing upon its contents, and of asserting after due perusal that it is calculated to be admirably serviceable to every class of scholars and learners. And this assertion is based upon the fact that it is a by no means one-sided edition, and that it looks as with the hundred eyes of Argus, here, there, and everywhere, to keep the reader from straying. In a

CATENA CLASSICORUM—Opinions of the Press.

concise and succinct style of English annotation, forming the best substitute for the time-honoured Latin notes which had so much to do with making good scholars in days of yore, Mr. Jebb keeps a steady eye for all questions of grammar, construction, scholarship, and philology, and handles these as they arise with a helpful and sufficient precision. In matters of grammar and syntax his practice for the most part is to refer his reader to the proper section of Madvig's 'Manual of Greek Syntax;' nor does he ever waste space and time in explaining a construction, unless it be such an one as is not satisfactorily dealt with in the grammars of Madvig or Jelf. Experience as a pupil and a teacher has probably taught him the value of the wholesome task of hunting out a grammar reference for oneself, instead of finding it handy for slurring over, amidst the hundred and one pieces of information in a voluminous foot-note. But whenever there occurs any peculiarity of construction, which is hard to reconcile to the accepted usage, it is Mr. Jebb's general practice to be ready at hand with manful assistance."—*Contemporary Review.*

"Mr. Jebb has produced a work which will be read with interest and profit by the most advanced scholar, as it contains, in a compact form, not only a careful summary of the labours of preceding editors, but also many acute and ingenious original remarks. We do not know whether the matter or the manner of this excellent commentary is deserving of the higher praise: the skill with which Mr. Jebb has avoided, on the one hand, the wearisome prolixity of the Germans, and on the other the jejune brevity of the Porsonian critics, or the versatility which has enabled him in turn to elucidate the plots, to explain the verbal difficulties, and to illustrate the idioms of his author. All this, by a studious economy of space and a remarkable precision of expression, he has done for the 'Ajax' in a volume of some 200 pages."—*Athenæum.*

Mr. Simcox's Juvenal.

"Of Mr. Simcox's 'Juvenal' we can only speak in terms of the highest commendation, as a simple, unpretending work, admirably adapted to the wants of the school-boy or of a college pass-man. It is clear, concise, and scrupulously honest in shirking no real difficulty. The pointed epigrammatic hits of the satirist are every where well brought out, and the notes really are what they profess to be, explanatory in the best sense of the term."—*London Review.*

"This is a link in the *Catena Classicorum* to which the attention of our readers has been more than once directed as a good Series of Classical works for School and College purposes. The Introduction is a very comprehensive and able account of Juvenal, his satires, and the manuscripts."—*Athenæum.*

"This is a very original and enjoyable Edition of one of our favourite classics."—*Spectator.*

"Every class of readers—those who use Mr. Simcox as their sole interpreter, and those who supplement larger editions by his concise matter—will alike find interest and careful research in his able Preface. This indeed we should call the great feature of his book. The three facts which sum up Juvenal's history so far as we know it are soon despatched; but the internal evidence both as to the dates of his writing and publishing his Satires, and as to his character as a writer, occupy some fifteen or twenty pages, which will repay methodical study."—*Churchman.*

London, Oxford, and Cambridge

CATENA CLASSICORUM—Opinions of the Press.

Mr. Bigg's Thucydides.

"Mr. Bigg in his 'Thucydides' prefixes an analysis to each book, and an admirable introduction to the whole work, containing full information as to all that is known or related of Thucydides, and the date at which he wrote, followed by a very masterly critique on some of his characteristics as a writer." —*Athenæum.*

"While disclaiming absolute originality in his book, Mr. Bigg has so thoroughly digested the works of so many eminent predecessors in the same field, and is evidently on terms of such intimacy with his author as perforce to inspire confidence. A well-pondered and well-written introduction has formed a part of each link in the 'Catena' hitherto published, and Mr. Bigg, in addition to a general introduction, has given us an essay on 'Some Characteristics of Thucydides,' which no one can read without being impressed with the learning and judgment brought to bear on the subject."—*Standard.*

"We need hardly say that these books are carefully edited; the reputation of the editor is an assurance on this point. If the rest of the history is edited with equal care, it must become the standard book for school and college purposes."—*John Bull.*

"Mr. Bigg first discusses the facts of the life of Thucydides, then passes to an examination into the date at which Thucydides wrote; and in the third section expatiates on some characteristics of Thucydides. These essays are remarkably well written, are judicious in their opinions, and are calculated to give the student much insight into the work of Thucydides, and its relation to his own times, and to the works of subsequent historians."—*Museum.*

Mr. Heslop's Demosthenes.

"The usual introduction has in this case been dispensed with. The reader is referred to the works of Grote and Thirlwall for information on such points of history as arise out of these famous orations, and on points of critical scholarship to 'Madvig's Grammar,' where that is available, while copious acknowledgments are made to those commentators on whose works Mr. Heslop has based his own. Mr. Heslop's editions are, however, no mere compilations. That the points required in an oratorical style differ materially from those in an historical style, will scarcely be questioned, and accordingly we find that Mr. Heslop has given special care to those characteristics of style as well as of language, which constitute Demosthenes the very first of classic orators."—*Standard.*

"We must call attention to New Editions of various classics, in the excellent 'Catena Classicorum' series. The reputation and high standing of the editors are the best guarantees for the accuracy and scholarship of the notes." —*Westminster Review.*

"The notes are thoroughly good, so far as they go. Mr. Heslop has carefully digested the best foreign commentaries, and his notes are for the most part judicious extracts from them."—*Museum.*

"The annotations are scarcely less to be commended for the exclusion of superfluous matter than for the excellence of what is supplied. Well-known works are not quoted, but simply referred to, and information which ought to have been previously acquired is omitted."—*Athenæum.*

London, Oxford, and Cambridge

CATENA CLASSICORUM—Opinions of the Press.
Mr. Green's Aristophanes.

"Mr. Green has discharged his part of the work with uncommon skill and ability. The notes show a thorough study of the two Plays, an independent judgment in the interpretation of the poet, and a wealth of illustration, from which the Editor draws whenever it is necessary."—*Museum*.

"Mr. Green's admirable Introduction to 'The Clouds' of the celebrated comic poet deserves a careful perusal, as it contains an accurate analysis and many original comments on this remarkable play. The text is prefaced by a table of readings of Dindorf and Meineke, which will be of great service to students who wish to indulge in verbal criticism. The notes are copious and lucid, and the volume will be found useful for school and college purposes, and admirably adapted for private reading."—*Examiner*.

"Mr. Green furnishes an excellent Introduction to 'The Clouds' of Aristophanes, explaining the circumstances under which it was produced, and ably discussing the probable object of the author in writing it, which he considers to have been to put down the Sophists, a class whom Aristophanes thought dangerous to the morals of the community, and therefore caricatured in the person of Socrates,—not unnaturally, though irreverently, choosing him as their representative. —*Athenæum*.

Mr. Sandy's Isocrates.

"Isocrates has not received the attention to which the simplicity of his style and the purity of his Attic language entitle him as a means of education. Now that we have so admirable an edition of two of his Works best adapted for such a purpose, there will no longer be any excuse for this neglect. For carefulness and thoroughness of editing, it will bear comparison with the best, whether English or foreign. Besides an ample supply of exhaustive notes of rare excellence, we find in it valuable remarks on the style of Isocrates and the state of the text, a table of various readings, a list of editions, and a special introduction to each piece. As in other editions of this series, short summaries of the argument are inserted in suitable places, and will be found of great service to the student. The commentary embraces explanations of difficult passages, with instructive remarks on grammatical usages, and the derivation and meanings of words illustrated by quotations and references." —*Athenæum*.

"This Work deserves the warmest welcome for several reasons. In the first place, it is an attempt to introduce Isocrates into our schools, and this attempt deserves encouragement. The *Ad Demonicum* is very easy Greek. It is good Greek. And it is reading of a healthy nature for boys. The practical wisdom of the Greeks is in many respects fitted to the capacities of boys; and if books containing this wisdom are read in schools, along with others of a historical and poetical nature, they will be felt to be far from dry. Then the Editor has done every thing that an editor should do. We have a series of short introductory essays; on the style of Isocrates, on the text, on the *Ad Demonicum*, and on the *Panegyricus*. These are characterized by sound sense, wide and thorough learning, and the capability of presenting thoughts clearly and well."—*Museum*.

"By editing Isocrates Mr. Sandys does good service to students and teachers of Greek Prose. He places in our hands in a convenient form an author who will be found of great use in public schools, where he has been hitherto almost unknown. . . . Mr. Sandys worthily sustains as a commentator the name which he has already won. The historical notes are good, clear, and concise; the grammatical notes scholar-like and practically useful. Many will be welcome alike to master and pupil."—*Cambridge University Gazette*.

London, Oxford, and Cambridge

CATENA CLASSICORUM.

The following Parts are in course of preparation:—

PLATONIS PHAEDO,
Edited by ALFRED BARRY, D.D. late Fellow of Trinity College, Cambridge; Principal of King's College, London.

DEMOSTHENIS ORATIONES PUBLICAE,
Edited by G. H. HESLOP, M.A. late Fellow and Assistant Tutor of Queen's College, Oxford; Head Master of St. Bees.
[Part III. De Falsâ Legatione.

MARTIALIS EPIGRAMMATA,
Edited by GEORGE BUTLER, M.A. Principal of Liverpool College; late Fellow of Exeter College, Oxford.

DEMOSTHENIS ORATIONES PRIVATAE,
Edited by ARTHUR HOLMES, M.A. Fellow and Lecturer of Clare College, Cambridge. [Part I. De Coronâ.

HOMERI ILIAS,
Edited by S. H. REYNOLDS, M.A. Fellow and Tutor of Brasenose College, Oxford. [Vol. I. Books I. to XII.

HORATI OPERA,
Edited by J. M. MARSHALL, M.A. Fellow and late Lecturer of Brasenose College, Oxford; one of the Masters in Clifton College.

TERENTI COMOEDIAE,
Edited by T. L. PAPILLON, M.A. Fellow and Classical Lecturer of Merton College, Oxford. [Part I. Andria et Eunuchus.

HERODOTI HISTORIA,
Edited by H. G. WOODS, M.A. Fellow and Tutor of Trinity College, Oxford.

TACITI HISTORIAE,
Edited by W. H. SIMCOX, M.A. Fellow and Lecturer of Queen's College, Oxford.

OVIDI TRISTIA,
Edited by OSCAR BROWNING, M.A. Fellow of King's College, Cambridge; and Assistant Master at Eton College.

CICERONIS ORATIONES,
Edited by CHARLES EDWARD GRAVES, M.A. Classical Lecturer and late Fellow of St. John's College, Cambridge.
[Part I. Pro P. Sextio.

THEOPHRASTI CHARACTERES,
Edited by A. PRETOR, M.A. of Trinity College, Cambridge; Classical Lecturer of Trinity Hall.

London, Oxford, and Cambridge